Behold Our God

Behold Our God

Contemplative Theology for the Soul

Justin Mandela Roberts

WIPF & STOCK · Eugene, Oregon

BEHOLD OUR GOD
Contemplative Theology for the Soul

Copyright © 2014 Justin Mandela Roberts. All rights reserved. Except for brief quotations in critical publications or reviews, no part of this book may be reproduced in any manner without prior written permission from the publisher. Write: Permissions. Wipf and Stock Publishers, 199 W. 8th Ave., Suite 3, Eugene, OR 97401.

Wipf and Stock
An Imprint of Wipf and Stock Publishers
199 W. 8th Ave., Suite 3
Eugene, OR 97401

www.wipfandstock.com

ISBN 13: 978-1-62564-659-0

Manufactured in the U.S.A. 07/23/2014

To Jordon Hanley,

Your company fed my soul in a way
I will always regard as gift.

Contents

Preface | ix
Acknowledgments | xi
Introduction | xiii

1 God | 1
2 Image | 10
3 Sin | 18
4 Atonement | 27
5 Resurrection | 36
6 Word | 45
7 Sacrament | 52
8 Church | 60
9 Eschatology | 69
10 Prolegomena | 76
Epilogue | 85

Appendix A
On the Cruciformity of Knowledge: A Sermon | 87

Appendix B
Gregory of Nyssa: A Sermon on the Sixth Beatitude | 94

Bibliography | 101

Preface

IF THE READER IS inclined to draw a sharp distinction between theology and spirituality then they shall be disappointed. While both are substantial themes that warrant thoroughness and rigor in their investigation, the purpose of the present work cannot afford to so limit itself. And if this book should be considered an investigation of any kind than it is an investigation of a particular sort. For in as much as it invokes "God" it conflicts with unimaginative reading that fails to perceive the reality beyond the discourse. It is not a lexical exercise with encyclopedic ends, rather its "content" will be misconstrued if the actuality of those realities in question is not evidently prominent.

In so doing it is not the intention to use Christian doctrine to supplement spiritual nourishment nor invite personal involvement to justify theology. Rather, the attempt is to enmesh the reader into the phenomenon of being, the dynamism of existence. The purpose is to facilitate the perpetual reconsideration of the wonder of things. Therefore this work does not relate personal experience and dogmatic confession for the sake of a certain end, but excites the rhapsody of God and the profundity of life. And as a byproduct it makes a case for reverence as the dwelling of knowledge. "One thing have I asked of the LORD, that will I seek after; that I may dwell in the house of the LORD all the days of my life, to gaze upon the beauty of the LORD" (Ps 27:4 ESV).

However, we are often prone to forgetting, the innocence of life's immediacy weathered by the passing of time. Wonder is a fragile thing that struggles for breath in the habits, environment, and perhaps slothfulness of our vision. We require guidance in

Preface

order to see the world. Moreover, we are given to a time that is less hospital to transcendental ends than others. It is for this reason that a book such as this may be helpful. It takes small subtle steps, but steps nonetheless. Thus we anticipate the day it shall be said, "Behold, this is our God" (Isa 25:9 ESV).

Acknowledgments

This book is the fruit of prayer, not the praying designated by the liturgical act but the seeing that refuses to diminish life. It is a way of being that robs the mundane and occasions a weighty *sanctum*. No one in my life has so demonstrated such a praying existence as Hans Boersma of Regent College, whose example I regard in the utmost. Therefore this book is more accurately the fruit of others' praying.

Moreover, my dear friend Phil Cotnoir is in no uncertain way responsible for having an idea manifest into the present volume. From jotted notes to a formatted manuscript, Phil has seen this work through and poignantly spoken in ways only possible by the genuine truthfulness that proper listening requires. There were also many others who read in different portions, and at different times, part of this manuscript and provided invaluable input, for their openness and insights I am truly indebted.

I would also like to express my gratitude for those at Wipf and Stock Publishers. All their dealing has been delightfully efficient and understanding, and it is my pleasure to contribute to their robust collection.

Finally, there are no words which properly recognize my wife Abbie, whose unending selflessness continues to make our life possible.

Introduction

Speaking of God

How is it that *we* might speak of God, and with the still greater contention that *he* might speak to us? Regarding the former, we may be tempted to ruminate theoretically upon the possibility and nature of God. However, the latter concerns that arresting presence without which all speculation is merely the cataloging of ideas. For it is precisely the advent of God's speaking to us that transfigures analysis into beholding, thought into contemplation. And thus in our speaking, we are asked of the jury to testify not on the condition of being experts but of being *witnesses*.

"This Is My Sworn Testimony"

The years leading up to my first significant interaction with the Christian faith were characterized by nothing less than an explicit search for meaning. In a process of maturation, I found myself progressing from adolescent curiosity, to a disciplined student of influential thinkers, and even to a conscientious pursuer of a novel concept called "love." Having taken a degree of joy in the liberty entailed in getting to decide which perspective was good, true, and beautiful, there was somewhat of an ideological clash with the very particular, and seemingly ordinary, thing that was Christianity.

It was in a secondary school class that I first met two particular individuals who would have a unique influence on my life: one

Introduction

the teacher himself, and the other a friend and classmate. I do not recall exactly how or why we ever initiated talk of a religious nature; though, I was always given to discussing such things, and have no surprise that in some way it came up. What I do recall was that in the early stages of our conversing, I was rather convinced that these people were somewhat simple minded, and oddly loyal to what I thought was an outdated and archaic cultural artifact.

As time went on, our discussion grew in complexity and developed relationally. They began to share increasingly genuine responses that were more than conversational formulae. I began to learn of their struggles, their tumultuous pasts, and all along the way I felt refreshed by their commitment and care toward me—what I now would call "knowing them by their love" (cf. John 13:34–35).

I distinctly recall being particularly unforgiving in relation to the argumentation and logic which we exchanged. I would pour on heaps of charges and critiques—some of which I did not even find personally convincing—without demonstrating any indication that I had great sympathy, and even respect, toward them. I would return home from class with the conviction that though they did not always provide answers that would claim victory in debate, I nevertheless believed they held real estate in a world more interesting than my own.

Consider the following analogy. There is an exchange between two people: the one has a great passion for the arts, yet has limited experience and no technical training; the other is a student of fine arts with aspirations to become a great art critic. As the conversation goes on, the passionate one makes an effort to communicate the nature of a recent work she has encountered; by inflecting vocal tone, using wild and at times contrary physical descriptions, and referring to vibrant but unclear personal experiences, she exudes enthusiasm—yet without the resources of critical discourse. While no insignificant amount of time passes, the two continue back and forth in an attempt to clarify just what this young woman has seen. Over the course of the dialogue, through laborious investment of time and effort, the critic begins to get a sense of that which the

Introduction

woman saw. In fact, through the barrage of information thrown at him, he comes to discern that she has not witnessed any particular painting, no; she has witnessed a masterpiece, and now her capacity to articulate it has failed her.

The conclusion of my own account finds a progressively interested inquirer confronted by a masterpiece at which his own efforts of explication fail also; and he has been fumbling about in the attempt to explain it ever since. The success, and possibility, of communicating with another regarding the Father, Son, and Spirit is not dependent upon—so much—one's capacity to articulate, but upon whether or not they have seen the masterpiece.

The Journey (?)

Much has been made of the journey that is the spiritual life; many of us are accustomed to this analogy, and we may even be familiar with the basic contours of the map. For all that has been written on the nature of this endeavor, regarding the strategies, resources, and mindset required, there are nevertheless fewer works which contribute to shaping the venture itself. What is it that makes a journey a journey, and not a casual walk through easy terrain?

The purpose of this work is to provide something of the substance and content that is so integral to anything that might be called "spiritual formation"; the material herein will be meditative upon the sustenance of contemplation—a resource which makes worship of God increasingly intelligible. The content follows many of the central themes of Christian theology. There are many advantages to this outline: it provides a condensed encounter with the broad sweep of Christian thought; it corresponds topically with the material given to the training of ministers and scholars, and thereby provides supplementary material which is not an overwhelming addition; and by weaving the often separated emphases of various theological disciplines, it allows the reader to be encouraged that there is indeed life within what can be overwhelming and tedious discussion.

Introduction

Because this book attempts to introduce something of a "contemplative" vantage to theological reflection in a time less familiar with such approaches, it seems appropriate to provide two sermons that go some way in demonstrating what this vantage might look like "on the ground," as it were (see appendix A and B). The first, "On the Cruciformity of Knowledge," is my own; it integrates many of the themes found throughout this work and employs them within a generally brazen call to discipleship. The second, "Gregory of Nyssa: A Sermon on the Sixth Beatitude," is a reflection on church father Gregory of Nyssa's sermon, which compliments the first as a decidedly more "spiritual" and interior meditation. The hope is that these two pieces inform the practical range of "contemplative theology," a way of seeing advocated throughout Christianity's rich tradition.

The prayer which undergirds the formation of this piece, and provides the *telos* of its chapters, is that its reader might be touched personally, inspired spiritually, and guided theologically; and while its end is to affect the soul, it is nevertheless conceptual and cerebral by nature.

And the Life Was the Light of the World

We have seen the "image of the invisible God" (cf. Col 1:15) in the face of Christ, Son of the Father, anointed and quickened in the Spirit. And it is by the light of this lamp that the whole world has become visible. For theology is simply finding new ways to say, "And thus it is with Christ." It is this theology, always and ever doxology, which rightly beckons worship of God: "My soul longs, yes, faints for the courts of the LORD; my heart and flesh sing for joy to the living God" (Ps 84:2). Therefore in what follows one will find therein my clumsy analysis, my infantile experience, my solemn testimony: "For Thou hast made us for Thyself and our hearts are restless till they rest in Thee."[1]

---

1. Augustine, *Confessions*, I.I.

Introduction

Mysteries such as these are not merely theoretical and theological; they are thoroughly practical. It makes a great difference to the act of contemplation whether I see myself as an isolated subject, who, albeit assisted by God's grace, endeavors to understand something of the mysteries of revelation; or whether, in faith, I have the conviction that my inadequate attempt to understand is supported by the wisdom of the Holy Spirit dwelling within me, that my acts of worship, petition and thanksgiving are borne along and remolded by the Spirit's infinite and eternal acts, in that ineffable union by which all human doing and being has been lifted up and plunged into the river of eternal life and love.

—HANS URS VON BALTHASAR[2]

2. *Prayer*, 76.

1
God

Holiness

IT IS IN THE place of aftermath that we are most ably equipped to speak to God's ineffable qualities. Should we have had no resources to draw from, nor encounter upon which to reflect, there would remain no certainty as to whether a thing called "God" is tangible. In other words, speech about God says more than its content suggests; it says, in addition, that God is—and it has likely suggested that God *is* majestic:

> Who is like you, O LORD, among the gods? Who is like you, majestic in holiness, awesome in splendor, doing wonders? (Moses' prayer, Exod 15:11[1])

> There is none holy like the LORD; there is none besides you; there is no rock like our God. (Hannah's prayer, 1 Sam 2:2 ESV)

> Then King David went in and sat before the Lord, and said, "Who am I, O LORD GOD . . . there is no one like you, and there is no God besides you, according to all that we have heard with our ears." (David's prayer, 2 Sam 7:18, 22)

---

1. Unless otherwise noted, all Scripture citations are from the NRSV.

Behold Our God

> Ascribe to the Lord the glory due his name; worship the Lord in the splendor of holiness. . . . The voice of the Lord is powerful; the voice of the Lord is full of majesty. (David's prayer, Ps 29:2, 4 ESV)

> I saw the Lord sitting upon a throne. . . . And one called to another and said: "Holy, holy, holy is the Lord of hosts; the whole earth is full of his glory!" . . . And I said: "Woe is me! For I am lost; for I am a man of unclean lips." (Isaiah's vision, Isa 6:1, 3, 5 ESV)

There are few Christian impulses more natural than to ascribe, at least by means of verbal attestation, the descriptors of glory, majesty, and holiness to God. As an infant might correspond its appetite with its mother's breast, *doing before learning*, so too does the Christian name God as the Holy One, often *ascribing before knowing*. In as much as the infant might grow up to harvest a plenty by the toil and fruit of its own labor, so the Christian must grow up to labor and toil the harvests of God's holiness, the riches of his splendor.

It is this very longstanding tradition, that of naming God and speaking with an almost untenable familiarity with the opaque and abstract characteristics of the divine, which is now and has always been in danger of extinction. Its critics remain many, while its progression unrestrained and its credibility uncertain. How in fact does the dark and inscrutable nature of "holiness" make itself known to a being finite, fleeting, and frail, to say the very least? Unclear and problematic is this query to be sure. And yet, its tumultuous pathway has neither stopped travelers from treading it nor eliminated what seems to be compelling alternatives to a bewildered shoulder shrugging.

The answer, the unimpressive answer, is that human speech about ineffable qualities is rooted in the comprehensive horizon of that which the Christian has *beheld*. Speaking more than is obvious the psalmist says, "I have set the LORD always before me" (Ps 16:8).

Before we venture further, let us be assured what this cannot mean. It cannot mean that God is most genuinely perceived through a distilled experience which is thought to be a purified form: whether it be called dependence, angst, moral superiority, piety, logic, or subject. Moreover, it cannot require the full explication of its interior workings, whether epistemologically or ontologically (regarding knowledge and being). We are, in some way, called to speak with just such a humility as is appropriate for recipients of mercy. For we have not the achievement of garnering our faculties for the purpose of solving once and for all the God question; rather our faculties have been enlisted for the teleological service of *beholding* by the sheer *is-ness* of God. In other words, it is not *the possibility of speech* about God which makes him present to us, it is the presence of *God* who makes theo-logical speech possible. Beholding is forever in the position of aftermath.

In the passages cited above, it comes to be no coincidence that the most poignant confessions of God's holiness are to be found in the context of prayer. One might be interested to ask if prayer, as a human contribution, is a work and orientation which rightly organizes the heart and mind to perceive God. But again, the opposite is the case. In all that is the glorious and terrible presence of God, its recipients are curtailed into an inevitable counterpart: a disposition called "prayer."

Mystery

The presence that "God" names is so appropriately called "mysterious"; and yet how much naiveté, and poor logic, is passed under the guise of mystery. Sparing all that can, and should, be said about this tantalizing concept, let us say this much: mystery at least captures the duality that is God's infinite distance presented at an uneasy proximity. And it is likely that while this notion gambles with the limitations of intelligibility, the believer will be all too familiar with it. But before we too confidently attribute to the divine what is deemed self-evident, perhaps we should tend the distinctive features of God's presence as that which instructs any and all thought in the vicinity of mystery.

Behold Our God

That mystery is not most accurately known in the abyss of contemplative darkness, but rather in the radiance of the light of God:

> Long ago God spoke to our ancestors in many and various ways by the prophets, but in these last days he has spoken to us by a Son, whom he appointed heir of all things, through whom he also created the worlds. He is the reflection of God's glory and the exact imprint of God's very being, and he sustains all things by his powerful word. (Heb 1:1-3)

So soon are we led from the contours of God's Being to the one with dusty feet roaming Nazareth, from the universal to the particular. And the Christian must again traverse this path should they at any point rightly contest the ineffable.

It is at this point which we might learn most from Luther. Should we be given to embellished inventing or rather put off from tending the riches of God's mysterious depths, we are given a corrective and anchor that is at once the infinite distance of God at an uneasy proximity, namely the person of Jesus. As Luther cared to point out, God—a term with as much diversity and abuse as can be imagined—is said to be precisely where he ought not to be. God is found in that place we might look should someone mention failure, abandonment, condemnation, and suffering. Because of this, we might say God is hidden, and yet hidden in plain sight. "He deserves to be called a theologian . . . who comprehends the visible things of God seen through suffering and the cross."[2] We see just such a prioritization in that of Dietrich Bonhoeffer: "In the incarnation, God reveals himself without concealment. Not the Logos, the Godhead or the manhood of Christ, but the whole person of the God-man is in the humiliation. He veils himself in the concealment of this scandal."[3]

What then is to be learned from this most interesting development? All too much. On the one hand we must ask, "Under whose account then does the verdict of Jesus' condemnation fall?" On the other, "What reading of Jesus makes possible the conclusion

2. Luther, *Heidelberg Disputation*, thesis #20, in Grimm, *Luther's Works*.
3. Bonhoeffer, *Christology*, 110–11.

that God is love?" In other words, God's peculiar appearance in Jesus forever determines the shape of our knowledge. The believer therefore is banned from spewing words such as "justice," "holiness," and "love" in the unfettered manner of self-flattery. No longer is the inclination to invent acceptable; rather the only thing which remains is to *behold*.

The Lord Is Likened Unto . . .

It is to one's great regret that in Christian tradition the insistence upon Christ's scandalous particularity and the attestation of the glories of God which flow through creation have been less than harmonious dancing partners: that is, a theology of the cross and a theology encompassing of nature. Whether it is the creation which is neglected for more salvific enterprises, or the Word under romantic sympathies, there seems to be a parched land of theological practice in this important and fluid relationship. How might we effortlessly weave the mundane with the sublime, the grounded with the euphoric? For us, it just might begin at the well.

"Wearied as he was from his journey," Jesus sat beside the well in the heat of the day (John 4:6 ESV[4]). As a Samaritan woman approached to draw water, Jesus extended a gesture of great surprise, to share a drink from her hand. For this Samaritan was not to be a contemporary companion of Jewish men. And even at this point, the subtle camaraderie between the two over their mutual desire for nourishment is not without its importance. Furthermore, Jesus introduces the curious suggestion that if she knew the gift of God, and who it is who stands before her, than she would have received "living water" upon her request (v. 10). For the one who shares our thirst knows with ceaseless compassion the craving of our souls, each being not far removed from the other. Yet, the woman questions the resources at his disposal, given that the well is "deep." How much greater still is the depth belonging to the heart. Moreover Jesus identifies this woman's questionable marital past in the

---

4. All quotations from John 4 are taken from the ESV.

attempt to make clear that the routinized tending to this well is the lesser of concerns. Had she known the sweet taste of eternal life, she would know within herself a well springing to newness. And in the spirit of protest still, she contests the historic differences she, a Samaritan, shares with this Jewish man. Jesus resolves her narrow-sighted concerns as he proclaims that true worshippers will not be confined to a certain mountain, but will enjoy the life of God through Spirit in truth—after all, the one who would reveal all things is the one to whom she speaks.

What exactly compelled this woman as she progressed back and forth in dialogue with Jesus is not entirely clear, neither is it entirely relevant; the woman left in an altogether different state from which she arrived. A local woman tending the well in the heat of the day, perhaps in fear of her peers and particularly concerned with material matters, "left her water jar and went away into town and spoke to the people" (v. 28). And with poetic symmetry, the disciples respond with shock as they return to the scene; when the disciples offer Jesus food to eat, he says, "My food is to do the will of him who sent me and to accomplish his work" (v. 34).

"As a deer pants for flowing streams, so pants my soul for you, O God" (Ps 42:1 ESV). At the conclusion of Scripture, "the Spirit and the Bride say, 'Come.' And let the one who hears say, 'Come.' And let the one who is thirsty come; let the one who desires take the water of life without price" (Rev 22:17 ESV). For some, this is an expression and prayer commensurate with their most sincere desires, for others it is not always known *that* they are thirsty, or rather for *what* they thirst.

When it comes to the satisfactions we experience on earth, the quenching of thirst for instance, there is a distinct limitation. While our thirst may be all consuming at times, the abundance of water—that which we crave—nullifies our thirst; we become no longer interested.

In the life of God, we see the mutual coexistence of thirst, satisfaction, and abundance. In ordinary circumstances, abundance quenches thirst which incrementally diminishes the satisfaction; yet in the triune, perichoretic, life of the divine, one's desire and

God

affection is ever and always growing; this in turn is met by the eternal resource that is his Being, which makes possible the existence of sustained satisfaction. "You make known to me the path of life; in your presence there is fullness of joy; at your right hand are pleasures forevermore" (Ps 16:11 ESV).

That being said, is one to trust the cravings and longing of the soul? Are we permitted to ascribe unto the Lord any and all depictions of self-fulfillment? The concern with relating our desires with the Being of God, and therefore representation of God in creation, is steadied by a tradition of prayer in the Psalms. And as we have witnessed at the well, Jesus Christ spoke and taught with ease concerning the relationship of the corruptible and the incorruptible. In this way, we are not concerned with constructing an image which coincides with the convenient desires of our lives; rather having beheld the Lord in the "splendor of holiness," the joys which we know from creation are understood first more accurately and consequently experienced in the light of their eternal counterpart. We no longer distinguish between the two, in so far as the blessings of life are linked to the fount from which they flow. "As a father has compassion on his children, so the Lord has compassion on those who fear him; for he knows how we are formed, he remembers that we are dust. The life of mortals is like grass, they flourish like a flower of the field; the wind blows over it and it is gone, and its place remembers it no more. But from everlasting to everlasting the Lord's love is with those who fear him" (Ps 103:13–17 ESV).

How curious that in "coming to Jesus," a quaint notion to be sure, we have travelled from well-side searching for water to declarations of God's splendor and back. Instructed by the great I AM who appeared in Nazareth, we are guided in our consideration and imagination. For creation can provide aid in our attempts to articulate the nature of God.

When something which surpasses comprehension is said of God, we may be at a loss in thinking of it abstractly; yet we might find that an object found in creation fits the linguistic character of that unique quality.

Behold Our God

What is known of the Trinity is not achieved on account of real firsthand experience which would make plain the nature of this mystery. There is however a vast collection in the Christian tradition—that is the tradition of Jesus Christ—which shapes the outer contours of what we might wish to say of God, and what we might regard as transgressing an essential component. God is distinguished in the three persons of Father, Son, and Spirit. However, language which ordinarily accompanies this threefold formula is not appropriate as this God is and has always been one. There is at once an inner relationship of mutual life. This life is not really still, or static, and yet it is not conducive to notions of change. Jesus spoke in terms which suggest something like a relationship of origination from the Father to the Son and Spirit, and still that concept of origination cannot nullify what has been said of the eternality of the Son and Spirit.

Perhaps our linguistic perils can be, at least temporarily, calmed as we consider the image of God as a raging fire. Standing attentive before a great fire, one is met by a small sense of fascination. Even at a distance its light flickers and draws attention. Standing near, its glow is something of a dance as the flames intertwine. Those flames are distinguishable and yet never separate; the fire is a plurality within its singularity. Moreover, it appears to have a starting place, a movement, and a point of ceasing; but again, it sustains each of these characteristics in what is an unending generation and consummation at present. Could this be appropriately explained to the person who either has never seen a fire or is somehow lacking the perception required? Likely only in small, fragmentary, and unfulfilling pieces. Notice then the progression of conceptual and linguistic construction borne of a unique encounter with Jesus Christ and put to the service of spiritual nourishment and contemplation. Such an engagement with divine things does not suffer the superficiality of finding stretched allusions under every rock, but occupies the student, the lover, the contemplative with the One who never ceases to embrace and elude.

God

O Creator ineffable, who of the riches of Thy wisdom didst appoint three hierarchies of Angels and didst set them in wondrous order over the highest heavens, and who didst apportion the elements of the world most wisely: do Thou, who art in truth the fountain of light and wisdom, deign to shed upon the darkness of my understanding the rays of Thine infinite brightness, and remove far from me the twofold darkness in which I was born, namely, sin and ignorance. Do Thou, who givest speech to the tongues of little children, instruct my tongue and pour into my lips the grace of Thy benediction. Give me keenness of apprehension, capacity for remembering, method and ease in learning, insight in interpretation, and copious eloquence in speech. Instruct my beginning, direct my progress, and set Thy seal upon the finished work, Thou, who art true God and true Man, who livest and reignest world without end. Amen.

—THOMAS AQUINAS[5]

---

5. Taken from Pope Pius IX, encyclical *Studiorum Ducem*, June 29, 1923.

2
Image

> So God created humankind in his image, in the image of God he created them; male and female he created them.
>
> —GENESIS 1:27

> What are human beings that you are mindful of them, mortals that you care for them? Yet you have made them a little lower than God, and crowned them with glory and honor.
>
> —PSALM 8:4–5

FEW IDEAS HAVE IMPACTED the world like this one, its reception as liberating as it is tenuous. It is not a novel concept that God would be represented by an image nor that certain human beings should be designated as such. What is novel is the scope and shape of that image in the Christian tradition.

Understanding that human beings are created in the image of God has made boundary-crossing love possible, and failing to realize it has permitted the horrific and unimaginable. In those moments when human beings are looked upon as that which is less than human, this idea is invariably required. However, the great atrocities that have plagued our world are not merely the result of our failing to recognize this fact in others, it is also to falsely

Image

recognize it in ourselves. The *imago Dei* has provided the opportunity for many to "image" the full array of obscure and heinous deities produced from a corrupt imagination. And thus for some, the designation "image of God" wreaks with a self-serving arrogance and does little more than to legitimate humanity's narrative of oppression. Yet far from a desperate effort to "grasp" (cf. Phil 2:6–11) at control and power, we see in the true image a thoroughgoing willingness to relinquish them. For delight and self-giving gratuity are integral to the very essence of that image, and in so far as humanity shares in *that* nature are they properly "of God." Image bearing is not a feat performed nor a victory won, rather it is the possibility of love. Therefore at once meager and divine humanity is ever the work of love, an existence precluded from boasting with mercy emanating from the testimony of its being.

For dust is of no more noble heritage than that of the "beasts": as it says, "Then the LORD God formed man from the dust of the ground, and breathed into his nostrils the breath of life" (Gen 2:7). Humanity, borne from the same ground, shares with the beasts their mandate to increase and multiply—and with the same contingency as those who live by the fruit of the earth. God's creative work takes the shape of speaking light into darkness, life into lifelessness, and peace into hostility. And *this* is the narrative of God's people. The following rehearsal of Christian history illumines the pervasive and essential principle that all things (whether Jew or Gentile) owe their existence to God's benevolence, the gratuitous abundance of his good gifts.

"And God Said, 'Let There Be . . .'"

To begin, the universality of God's vision is made possible by his unfolded plan of redemption for, not merely the Jews but, the Gentiles. As the Apostle Peter addresses his readers, he reminds them that "once you were not a people, but now you are God's people; once you had not received mercy, but now you have received mercy" (1 Pet 2:10). Paul, likewise, expounds his "insight into the mystery of Christ, which was not made known to humankind in other generations as it has now been revealed to his holy apostles and prophets by the Spirit. This mystery is that the Gentiles are fellow heirs, members of the same body, and partakers of the promise in Christ Jesus through the gospel" (Eph 3:4–6). As "fellow heirs," our claim for privilege and boasting is of not.

This new "body," moreover, is given unity through a stunning while gracious event. The church is an entity made possible by being raised *with* Christ, the one billowing forth from death and hades. Our fate, being once confined to the man of dust, is taken up by the Son of Man: "The first man was from the earth, a man of dust; the second man is from heaven. As was the man of dust, so are those who are of the dust; and as is the man of heaven, so are those who are of heaven. Just as we have borne the image of the man of dust, we will also bear the image of the man of heaven" (1 Cor 15:47–49). Christ's resurrection is determinative in *form* and *content* for the life of the church: it exhibits God's capacity to initiate and his purposive means of redemption respectively.

This voluntary and unsolicited nature is evinced even in the beginning of Jesus' ministry, as we are again stuck by the proclivity of God to select an odd and unsavory bunch. His chosen disciples are an assortment of fisherman, tax collectors, and the like. Christ demonstrates from the outset the way in which he can make much of little, and fisherman fishers of persons (Mark 1:17).

And in defiance of all human achievements, the savior of the world comes as one from on high. God's speaking forth into the womb should create no less than life in the pure and virgin servant that is Mary, Mother of God: "For the child conceived in her is from the Holy Spirit" (Matt 1:20). We are due no congratulatory celebration for stewarding a messiah in our midst. This "Immanuel" would be relevant to a people who, though released from exile, saw themselves as waiting for the true Servant who would bring peace—one to sit upon David's throne.

And yet not even king David escapes his humanity. For as Samuel observed the candidates before him, he considered the first of Jesse's many sons: "Surely the LORD's anointed is now before [him]" (1 Sam 16:6). But the LORD replied, "Do not look on his

Image

appearance or on the height of his stature, because I have rejected him; for the LORD does not see as mortals see; they look on the outward appearance, but the LORD looks on the heart" (1 Sam 16:7). The king was realized in the delayed selection of a young shepherd who would lead with a courageously vulnerable faith in God.

And not too soon we remember just how it was that Samuel was born. For his life is owed to the muttered prayers of a desolate woman that found themselves before God: "'Hannah, why do you weep? Why do you not eat? Why is your heart sad?' . . . She made this vow: 'O Lord of hosts, if only you will look on the misery of your servant, and remember me, and not forget your servant, but will give to your servant a male child, then I will set him before you.' . . . The Lord remembered her. In due time Hannah conceived and bore a son. She named him Samuel, for she said, 'I have asked him of the Lord'" (1 Sam 1:8, 11, 19–20).

This is not unlike many of the great prophets and patriarchs. One considers the infamous scene of a weaved basket tumbling down the river, carrying within its embrace the infant who would one day confront the king of Egypt on God's behalf. For Moses himself was found abandoned for his own sake by a young woman, a rather ignoble origins as his life was spared by one who "took pity on him" (Exod 2:6). And the task to which Moses was called, that of leading forth a people out of captivity in Egypt, was remembered in the practice of feasting. Israel was never to forget *from whom* they were borne: "Observe the feast of unleavened bread, for on this very day I brought your [hosts] out of the land of Egypt" (Exod 12:17).

We think also of God's acts in and through Joseph who was stripped and abandoned by his own brothers; he was taken and thrown into a pit, only to be sold to a caravan of Ishmaelites for slavery (Gen 37:23–27). And yet God looked upon this one so forsaken and abandoned in prison and spoke to him.

Had these stories been true of those other than the great and central figures of the Christian narrative, it might have been possible to lose sight of the importance of their frailty; however, these accounts are in fact demonstrative of God's character, and thus explain his impatience with the entitled.

But perhaps the most compelling instances of God's imaginative mercy is Abraham himself. His resume lacks all the necessary requirements, and yet the degree to which he impacts history is unmatched. The entire course of redemption hinges on what God started, promised, and remained faithful toward in Abraham: for through this man, "all nations of the earth shall be blessed" (Gen 22:18).

What remains is the original, penetrating, and programmatic words, "In the beginning, God created the heavens and the earth. The earth was without form and void, and darkness was over the face of the deep. And the Spirit of God was hovering over the face of the waters. And God said, 'Let there be light,' and there was light" (Gen 1:1–3 ESV).

Therefore contrary to an oppressive ideology, the *imago Dei* is a benevolent work situated within a narrative of mercy: "What do you have that you did not receive?" (1 Cor 4:7).

"Growing Up in Every Way"

Thus, the *imago Dei* cannot be separated from the God that it reflects—the gracious, creative, and benevolent God; and this is reflected in the foundational stories Christians tell themselves. Therefore, we learn something of the image from the way in which it has been brought about. We see part of its nature in its beginning, an unnecessary though joyful movement flowing properly from the divine life itself. However, what is also true of those stories is the necessity of maturation, a theme as critical to image bearing as any other.

What is antithetical to sobriety and reason is that basal orientation toward selfishness, whether it be the simple instinctive response of a young child or the more severe impulse to acquire and dominate. As creatures seeking security, there is no end to our capacity to weigh, measure, and commodify the features of life. In fact there is no act pious or otherwise that escapes our "productivity." Bonhoeffer explains the ability to use even confession itself, the exact repentance from the self-seeking in question, for one's own gain: should one do so, "it will become the final, most abominable, vicious, and impure prostitution of the heart; the act becomes an idle, lustful babbling. Confession as a pious work is an invention of the devil."[1] Anyone familiar with the spiritual practices of the church and the fellowship of believers will be all too familiar with that profound aptitude for corruption, celebrating prestige and conjuring flattery. Therefore, it is no surprise that God beholds the "meek" and "pure of heart."

However, selfishness is antithetical to reason because it is damned. It is foreign to Being and fated by its own ignorance. For it is not long before the self-seeker (devoted to *my* good) will be confronted by an inconvenient reality: in as much as they are dedicated to their own ends they become incarcerated in the world around them, depending on that world to work in harmony with their loftiest aspirations. Self-seeking is complicated by others. Beckoned therefore to engage with the world, they are forced to consider the desires of others even if only to serve themselves. All the while, the world pushes back. And yet it is here that love graces our lives, where the distinction between the good for "others" and the good for ourselves is blurred. Love therefore is cognizant of harmony, the unity of *our* good.

As one's gaze stretches beyond the immediacy of self-interest, a once cunning awareness gives way to a considerate stewarding. In tending the soil, humanity knows not the luxury of a superior species but the responsibility of a reasoning being. Therefore humanity is elevated only to then care for the world, a relationship between intellect and charity that is derivative of God's essence: "The greatest among you must become like the youngest, and the leader like the one who serves. . . . I am among you as one who serves" (Luke 22:26–27).

The world has continued to inconvenience the selfish. And while the abhorrent may pillage and plunder, all are to reckon with the contingency of their lives. We are responsible to account for

---

1. Bonhoeffer, *Life Together*, 120.

Behold Our God

our place *under God* as well as *above creation*. Our attention to reality compels us to consider whence it came. Therefore, we are taken beyond ourselves to consider *the Good*. Expressed in the fabric of existence is the graciousness of life. The human person is so entirely unnecessary and thus excites wonder that there should be anything at all. Just as the nation of Israel had implicit in its existence the testimony to a work of God, so too does the human being inherently proclaim the otherness to which its being depends.

"From Glory to Glory"

As the original and blessed act of creation illumes the character of the image, so does the process of maturation itself. Humanity is first differentiated from God only to be drawn back to him, an intelligible rhythm of emanation and return. Moreover, the image reflects the procession and reciprocity of the Son, the Father's Word. And in growing up humanity does not simply mirror the divine Son, but shares in his very nature—partaking in infinite bliss. Embraced by the Spirit, humanity is analogous to the divine Being: at once other than God and yet actually participating in the eternal Logos. As Bonhoeffer explains, "[Maturation] is not achieved by dint of efforts 'to become like Jesus,' which is the way in which we usually interpret it. It is achieved only when the form of Jesus Christ itself works upon us in such a manner that it moulds our form in its own likeness."[2] This form—the *arche, reshith, logos*—permeates existence, providing a communicative presence to being. And thus we can think of creation as having a doxological rhetoric: "The heavens are telling the glory of God" (Ps 19:1) and "the whole earth is full of his glory" (Isa 6:3).

Now that we have beheld in Christ the "image of the invisible God" (Col 1:15), we "are being transformed into the same image from [glory to glory]" (2 Cor 3:18). And the *beholding* is not separate from the *transforming*; for in seeing him "as he is, . . . we will be like him" (1 John 3:2). Therefore, perfection is not a quality to

---

2. Bonhoeffer, *Ethics*, 80.

be attained once and for all, rather it is the unhindered and boundless motion of the soul toward the Good. It is unveiled beholding, stripped of all impediments. Thus the end of the image celebrates the love of its beginning, and ever proceeds in rhapsodic pursuit of the infinite. The Catholic theologian Erich Przywara describes life as "a never-ending . . . unveiling of the absolute infinite God in and above the never-ending . . . self-evolution of life in him."[3]

Therefore the proper nature of the *imago Dei*, delineated throughout its beginning, middle, and end, conflicts with all corrupt machinations. Image bearing is a dance in sync with the rhythm of reality, regarding all good things within Goodness itself. And thus the "image" will be *of God* in as much as it is the possibility of loving and being loved.

[Within the development of humanity] I cannot help thinking that the Next Step will be really new; it will go off in a direction you could never have dreamed of . . . if you care to talk in these terms, the Christian view is precisely that the Next Step has already appeared. And it is really new. It is not a change from brainy men to brainier men: it is a change that goes off in a totally different direction—a change from being creatures of God to being sons of God. The first instance appeared in Palestine two thousand years ago.

—C. S. LEWIS[4]

3. Przywara, *Polarity*, quoted in Johnson, *Karl Barth and the* Analogia Entis, 79.
4. *Mere Christianity*, 172.

3
Sin

"Sin is lurking at the door; its desire is for you, but you must master it."
Cain said to his brother Abel, "Let us go out to the field..."

—GENESIS 4:7–8

But exhort one another every day, as long as it is called "today," so that none of you may be hardened by the deceitfulness of sin.

—HEBREWS 3:13

For this perishable body must put on imperishability, and this mortal body must put on immortality. When this perishable body puts on imperishability, and this mortal body puts on immortality, then the saying that is written will be fulfilled: "Death has been swallowed up in victory." "Where, O death, is your victory? Where, O death, is your sting?" The sting of death is sin, and the power of sin is the law. But thanks be to God, who gives us the victory through our Lord Jesus Christ. Therefore, my beloved, be steadfast, immovable, always excelling in the work of the Lord, because you know that in the Lord your labor is not in vain.

—1 CORINTHIANS 15:52–58

Sin

WHERE ARE WE TO begin? Accounting for the woes and ways of a violent world is equally painful as it is difficult. Can we avoid that callous and, and at times imbecilic, speech which categorizes out of a need for self-justification? In other words, can we *name* sin without *explaining* it? It seems that we are obligated to so name, and yet never forget how truly out of sorts we are.

This entirely sensitive matter must be thought of in at least two ways, both of which require quite distinct ways of thinking. And as we find ourselves wedged between these two (necessary) perspectives, we notice just how similar our situation is to that of a physician. In order to be an effective and truthful practitioner, the physician must be competent in the theories surrounding medical practice—this is without question; and yet, that doctor will be cruel and tortuous if she is unable to delicately and thoughtfully tend the *people* in wisdom and in love. As persons, injured persons to be sure, we cannot afford to lack either theory or tenderness in our reflection on sin. And it is in a confessedly uncertain and yet rigorous condition that we must so name, and thereby name truthfully.

The Unnatural Nature of Sin

That loathsome plague we call "sin" is more than the sum of unpleasant and unfortunate realities; neither is it merely the opposition to what is good, or even God for that matter. Sin does not have a "place," and in some ways it is placelessness itself. It is not coeternally competitive with God, nor is it required to legitimate or define his essence: it is not the absence beside which presence is understood. It is in the most proper sense deprivation, a type of nonessential distortion, and it is thereby truly contingent. Its distorted (non)nature makes certain demands upon our considerations. We therefore cannot lament over sin as the fated and necessary equalizer which orders a tragic but reasonable harmony. Sin is senseless, violent, and parasitic: it was neither in the beginning nor will it be in the end.

It impedes on the existence, order, and nature of God's good and holy dwelling, another way of inciting "justice." Thus says the Lord, "Rejoice before the Lord your God—you and your sons and your daughters, your male and female slaves . . . the strangers, the orphans, and the widows who are among you—at the place that the Lord your God will choose as a dwelling for his name. Remember that you were a slave in Egypt, and diligently observe these statutes. . . . You must not distort justice; you must not show partiality. . . . Justice, and only justice, you shall pursue, so that you may live and occupy the land that the Lord your God is giving you" (Deut 16:11–12, 19–20). Justice therefore is the virtue of God's dwelling place, the character of those who live in and by his very life. For "the word of the Lord is upright, and all his work is done in faithfulness. He loves righteousness and justice; the earth is full of the steadfast love of the Lord" (Ps 33:4–5). Thus in failing to uphold widows and orphans, we commit an abominable and religious violence against the justice of Being, the love of God; in which case, all the ceremonial gestures offered unto the LORD are putrid (Isa 1:11–16): "But woe to you Pharisees! For you tithe mint and rue and herbs of all kinds, and neglect justice and the love of God; it is these you ought to have practiced, without neglecting the others" (Luke 11:42).

Evinced with penetrating clarity is the injustice resultant of king Nebuchadnezzar, a glorious display of pride's crime toward reality. For while walking on the "roof of the royal palace of Babylon" (Dan 4:29) assessing the grandeur of the nation, Nebuchadnezzar said, "Is this not magnificent Babylon, which I have built as a royal capital by my mighty power and for my glorious majesty?" (Dan 4:30).

He emerges as that platonic egotist who is embarrassingly ignorant of history's lessons, a blindness toward the past that is characteristic of his inability to perceive into the nature of life itself. And with "Babylon" exciting our memory of that villainous and apocalyptic whore (Rev 17:1–6), his grotesque arrogance makes us think that he has believed the tempter who awaits on the roofs

Sin

of life's palaces: "Then the devil led him up and showed him in an instant all the kingdoms of the world" (Luke 4:5).

Consequently he was driven from splendor to sharing his lot with the wild beasts of the field, a "lot" reminiscent of a carcass-draped couple and the prodigal son. And he "ate grass like oxen, and his body was bathed with the dew of heaven, until his hair grew as long as eagles' feathers and his nails became like birds' claws" (Dan 4:33). The easy transition from proud to primal invites our attention as they are differentiated only in kind not in substance.

Nebuchadnezzar's reason "returned" in the lifting up of his eyes to "heaven" saying, "I blessed . . . and praised and honored the one who lives forever" (Dan 4:35). It was precisely in the turning toward God, clothing himself with praise unto the LORD and reestablishing proper order and justice, that the divine dwelling was anemically made manifest.

And while some are tempted to level moral injunctions against the egotistic god of the Old Covenant—seeing in his protest of the proud a conflict of egos—we are to find tenderness, goodness, and justice as the divine impetus for ethical concern: "When justice is done, it is a joy to the righteous, but dismay to evildoers" (Prov 21:15). As God responds to a rebellious Israel, Isaiah declares that "the Lord waits to be gracious to you; therefore he will rise up to show mercy to you. For the Lord is a God of justice; blessed are all those who wait for him" (Isa 30:18). And the people of that heavenly Zion, that new Jerusalem, "shall weep no more," for the LORD "will surely be gracious to you at the sound of your cry" (Isa 30:19). And though for a time they are given the "bread of adversity and the water of affliction," their Teacher will not hide himself any longer (Isa 30:20): they shall eat and drink of that living and true source. It is just such a promise that makes the self-giving Christ intelligible; he "is my servant, whom I uphold, my chosen, in whom my soul delights; I have put my spirit upon him; he will bring forth justice to the nations" (Isa 42:1).

Lest we underestimate this relationship, that is the connection between ethical concern and God's love, it is worth noting that one of the most pervasive themes of God's works throughout history is his scandalous affirmation of those "outside the camp": we may think of Cyrus (Isa 45:1), Zacchaeus (Luke 19:1), or Saul the persecutor (Acts 9:1). And it has been inability to comprehend this scandalous orientation toward the "other" that has manifested in the cruel exercise of moral concern. For there is a proper and essential order to justice; and contrary to those stealthy Pharisees in the grainfields, "the sabbath was made for humankind, and not humankind for the sabbath" (Mark 2:27). The law is not by nature static because that for which it exists, namely sin, is neither eternal nor necessary. Law is invented, ad hoc, and due to hard-heartedness (Matt 19:8). Thus the true tone of ethical concern is desperation not tyranny. The prophets were demonstrative of this passion: "To us a single act of injustice—cheating in business, exploitation of the poor—is slight; to the prophets, a disaster. To us injustice is injurious to the welfare of the people; to the prophets it is a deathblow to existence; to us, an episode; to them, a catastrophe, a threat to the world."[1]

What Then Would You Have Me Do?

For all that must be said precisely about sin, there still remains the more acute and disturbing knowledge that transforms analysis into lament: that overcoming acquaintance in which there are no teachers, only mourners. For sin is the violence that has captured our love.

If we are to continue to address sin precisely than we are to confess truthfully, and that confession notices the unanswered longing "Why?" Elusive as it is concerning, we are *truthfully* beyond our depths. And yet, this is not the only occasion on which we are to navigate near paralyzing uncertainty. In fact, living well in the face of uncertainty is another way of referring to wisdom. And so long as we are obsessed with elucidating this tension as a prerequisite for joy, we will ever remain prisoners. There is an

---

1. Heschel, *Prophets*, 4.

Sin

audacity about the one who rejoices, and while pressed by the world—and ultimately without resolutions—this individual cannot help but ask her own question in return: "What then would you have me do?" For she knows as well as the next how troubling and displacing it is to stare blankly into the pervasive contradiction of finitude. And yet the "Why?" is poignant, stinging, and unrelenting. It is tempting to collect all the atrocities, inconsistencies, and chaos of the world for the end of usurping the throne of justice. No longer, it is thought, may "God" be allowed to reign—whether that God be an anthropological projection or in fact a true yet removed deity: "it" has been found unfit to serve.

And yet, can such grandiose aspirations of otherworldly tranquility truly escape the cycle of repetition—of revolt, corruption, subjugation? In other words, can the new regime satisfy the failings of the old? Where might we end up if we were to entrust our way to the basic and sensitive intuitions of our hearts? For God is judged on account of his apparent disregard for life and the suffering entailed therein; had God apprehended in wisdom and care the longsuffering of the earth, surely he would find such an existence pitiable. He, therefore, would concede the only possible conclusion to the finite predicament, that whatever "life" is it is not worth enduring existence: could any degree of bliss vindicate even one instantiation of the heinous sin we know too well? It completely and unreservedly could not. For what then do we await? For what do we hope? In a word: relief. We thereby look off to the fated yet welcomed messianic deliverer, death. We cannot help but think of the great many who may in fact delight in death over their lot in life, and thus we sympathize by wishing relief their way. And should we find temporary comfort, memory and imagination forever wed us to the inherent atrocities which plague existence. It seems by putting one foot in front of the other, our crusade on the divine judgment has procured the odd result of turning black into white. Setting sail on the ceiling of this backwards world, we have become ambassadors of destruction. Life has become the curse with God the primordial villain. Death therefore is the great comforter, the empathizing liberator.

But is this the picture we set out toward? Perhaps sin is in fact deceitful and "crafty," empowering enough to condemn and abandon. What if our discerning hearts were quickened by a sickness so translucid we extended and propagated the very evil which repulsed us? Can such a gospel be meaningfully distinguished from the works of sin and evil? Can such ambassadors be different than devils? Have we become enemies of life in the name of love? For "[sin] is necessarily a lie, surely, and is not the lie bound to lie to itself . . . is not this of the very essence of sin?"[2]

If we fail to attend this issue in wisdom, lending an ever intrigued ear to the slippery and subtle voice of doubt ("Did God actually say?" [Gen 3:1 ESV]), we shall taste of that destruction resultant from the proverbial "way" of unrighteousness: "The righteousness of the blameless keeps their ways straight, but the wicked fall by their own wickedness" (Prov 11:5). In our case, this is a falling and destruction wrought by decent intentions. However, it is often out of the innocent if presumptuous soil that the seeds of corruption grow: "You will not die" (Gen 3:4). And before long, after having discerned for ourselves that which is good for touching, tasting, and gaining knowledge, we become fellows with death, cursing "the day on which I was born" (Jer 20:14).

And as much as we may in fact resonate with such a cursing, it is often the other—vulnerable and in need of hope—that lures our best efforts forward, finding the resolution unto death ultimately unconvincing. We give company, love, and inspiration to others, and this gives us the excuse to exercise our highest aspirations for living; but that very offering is necessary for our survival—for the shadow of solitude mocks such sentiments. We often can only hear the truth as it is being ministered to others.

Again, searching for something that might pass for an explanation, we are just out of reach and know not solace. And while there are a variety of factors contributing to our ignorance, there is a specific and curious one that warrants attention. If angst was primarily human disorientation consequent of a logical tension than a fundamentally problem-solving approach would be appropriate.

---

2. Balthasar, *Prayer*, 232–33.

But as we can attest, the very same "problem" may surface with devastating effect at one time and be maintained under steady resolve at another. The solution rarely solves very much. Rather resolution is a kind of state, a strength or *ability* to so comprehend. It is less a matter for the mind and more a capacity of our being—ever mindful of the many things which contribute to this capacity.

That being said, our tenuous apprehension of God's goodness is not made possible by a kind of spiritual achievement (though in the truest sense, it could be said this way), rather it is those fortuitous instances of grace that enrapture us. Such scattered and fleeting moments of blissful forgetfulness offer us a glimmering, if temporary, hope in life after life. Whether it be the playful and easy tumbling of a mother's fresh cubs, the familiar togetherness which makes distance and time irrelevant, or the aromatic invitation of heavily roasted coffee, these moments communicate lofty and transcendent qualities proper to God and thereby may be thought as revelatory. They reveal precisely because they convince us that restoration is more than an illusion. With each new precious life, we are caught off guard and surprised by our celebration, a joy that teaches us to claim life as gift.

That They May Have Life

As experience would have it, controversy surrounds the appropriation of existence, the affirmation of being. That controversy, however, cannot be won by analytics, which is true to the nature of the issue. Rather, we require *permission*: permission synonymous with inspiration. By others' example we witness the courageous yet unjustified contradiction of corruption. In the process of seeing those examples they work to persuade and grant permission. And within that persuasion is the transferring of strength, as if we receive nourishment from the lives of others. Being so nourished we garner the strength to believe. And though we might simply witness another in their attempt to survive, enduring longsuffering with virtue, it is as though their suffering becomes *for us*—almost as if they begin to carry *our* burdens.

Behold Our God

> Thus, all reflection on the plight of finitude can be distilled into a sober moment of truth; however overwhelming and uncertain the issues become, there is Christ's question "Who do you say that I am?" (Mark 8:29). If Christ is God with us, than that is enough. It is enough because we can trust him, and because we trust him we have what is necessary for faith(fulness). We are given *permission* to live and *strength* to believe.

> But seeing the superiority of the incorruptible, I should have looked for You in that truth and have learned from it where evil is—that is learned the origin of the corruption by which Your substance cannot be violated. For there is no way in which corruption can affect our God, whether by His will or by necessity or by accident: for He is God, and what He wills is good, and Himself is Goodness; whereas to be corrupted is not good. Nor are You against Your will constrained to anything, for Your will is not greater than Your power. It would be greater, only if You were greater than Yourself: for God's will and God's power are alike God Himself. And what unlooked-for accident can befall You, since You know all things? No nature exists save because You know it. Why indeed should I multiply reasons to show that the substance which is God is not corruptible, since if it were, it would not be God?
>
> —AUGUSTINE[3]

---

3. *Confessions*, 7.4.

4
Atonement

Prologue

IF THEOLOGY IS QUEEN of the sciences, the atonement is the crown of theology. Every theological resource at our disposal is put to work in understanding this doctrine, and consequently this doctrine informs the whole of our life and thought. The atonement, namely the efficient work of Christ unto salvation, is often the summative paraphrase of the gospel; and as a result, it can be the victim of unreflective assumption and thoughtless repetition. Therefore, what is of greater value than rehearsing familiar clauses related to the cross is giving attention to the one(s) who served and suffered for God's purposes.

The cross is a phenomenon necessitated by a world plagued by horrific self-mutilation. On behalf of that world, the Psalmist vulnerably released his dereliction: "My God, my God, why have you forsaken me? Why are you so far from saving me, from the words of my groaning? O my God, I cry by day, but you do not answer, and by night, but I find no rest" (Ps 22: 1–2). Why indeed?

Act 1: Calling and Promise

Scene 1

A burning bush is a peculiar introduction to the God who will bring a nation to its knees, and yet this was the initial meeting between I AM and a disoriented, and slow-of-speech, Moses—who also happened to be a runaway convict (Exod 3:1–3). In the silence of Moses' astonishment God explained, "I have surely seen the affliction of my people who are in Egypt and have heard their cry because of their taskmasters"; and what is more, God revealed a most compassionate and hopeful response: "I know their sufferings, and I have come down to deliver them out of the land of the Egyptians" (Exod 3:7–8). Beyond something of a distanced and removed deity, the Lord responded with an invested interest. That place which he had envisioned for them was "good" and "broad," "flowing with milk and honey" (v. 8).

That being said, this land would not be acquired by means unfamiliar to a world of strife. The cry of the oppressed will be brought to a place of tearless comfort, so long as they are led by one called of God. As God said unto Moses, "I will send you to Pharaoh that you may bring my people, the children of Israel, out of Egypt" (v. 10). Moses, in the timidity and fear which rightly accompanies such a vocation, asked in return "Who am I?" And rather than offer words of consolation, or assurance of ease, God simply said "I will be with you" (v. 12).

Scene 2

Moving forward in time, while finding ourselves in familiar territory, God once again addressed an oppressed Israel in bondage. This time, it is from a place of exile that God's people cry out for his tender mercy and outstretched arm. God, willing to oblige, said to the people: "You were sold for nothing, and you shall be redeemed without money" (Isa 52:3); and while God's name was "despised" among the nations (v. 5), he would nevertheless publish peace and salvation.

This redemptive effort will be in like kind to that of Moses, and yet this will be a new "servant" who "shall act wisely" and be "high and lifted up" (v. 13 ESV): "There shall come forth a shoot from the stump of Jesse, and a branch from his roots shall bear fruit. And the Spirit of the Lord will rest upon him" (Isa 11:1–2 ESV). This one will be of no more admirable beginnings than that of Moses, having nothing attractive to his appearance. However, God will be mightily at work to fulfill that tearless hope in which even the wolf is said to dwell with the lamb (Isa 11:6).

Scene 3

"Immediately he saw the heavens being torn open and the Spirit descending on him like a dove. And a voice came from heaven, 'You are my beloved Son; with you I am well pleased'" (Mark 1:10–11 ESV). Israel's most tender hopes, which until this point have found only fragmentary satisfaction, are given new life. In fact, it is for this reason that the Son came, that an oppressed and desperate world might have life in abundance (John 10:10). That hope, however, is conditioned upon the work of a servant: "For even the Son of Man came not to be served but to serve, and to give his life as a ransom for many" (Mark 10:45 ESV). While in Isaiah we hear that God will purchase his people without cost to them, the vocation of leading the lost to a haven of rest will be trying, as has been the case.

Act 2: Testing and Trial

Scene 1

To Moses' demise, Pharaoh appears no more receptive to the Lord's intensions than he might have first hoped. God had sent Aaron and Moses, prepared with displays of grandeur, to Pharaoh, and he still would not concede. What is of interest here is that Pharaoh's resistance is toward that which is, for the reader at least, explicitly a work of God: "Then the Lord said to Moses . . . Then the Lord said to Moses . . . Then the Lord said to Moses" (Exod 7:8, 14, 19 ESV). The task breads confrontation by its very nature. The culmination of this tension is seen in Pharaoh's frustrated reaction to an emancipated Israel. He gathered his horses and pursued Israel to the point of no escape. It is by God's hand that his people passed through a parted sea to safety; and yet that story does not end, and Moses will have more to learn of bearing the burden of this people.

Scene 2

Having intimate familiarity with the account of God's great work in the exodus, Israel waited on another tested servant who would deliver them. Again, this elect one will find resistance to the work commissioned by God himself. "He was despised and rejected by men; a man of sorrows, and acquainted with grief; and as one from whom men hide their face he was despised" (Isa 53:3 ESV). "He was oppressed, and he was afflicted" (v. 7 ESV). And yet, the prophet assures his people that this torturous path is precisely what will make peace possible. Like Moses, this servant will wear the burdens of this people, namely oppression and affliction, as he works among them to bring forth the realization of shalom.

Scene 3

To some, Jesus' work of healing, giving, and forgiving was occasion for rejoicing; for others it was reason enough to protest. Jesus incited opposition as he gave sight to the blind, taught with authority, and pardoned the iniquity of sinners. Once again we see that it is no peripheral matter that was responsible for Jesus' persecution, it was rather the works integral to his vocation of bringing life, healing, and a new kingdom. In this way, Jesus endured opposition because it was an inevitable reaction to the work of God. The more he displayed the nature of his kingdom, the more affliction he

Atonement

incurred. The climax to this tension arrived when word came to Jesus that his message had attracted even the Greeks; in other words Jesus was now being placed on the world's stage, which meant the ramifications of his actions thereafter acquired a new magnitude: "Jesus answered them, 'The hour has come for the Son of Man to be gloried. Truly, truly, I say to you, unless a grain of wheat falls into the earth and dies, it remains alone; but if it dies, it bears much fruit. Whoever loves his life loses it, and whoever hates his life in this world will keep it for eternal life'" (John 12:23–25 ESV). Jesus hinted that in order to actualize the fruit it was required that he face death, and that anyone wishing to eat of that fruit must also taste of his death.

Act 3: Betrayal and Abandonment

Scene 1

Instead of adulation for his efforts, Moses found himself spread thin with a begrudging and complaining group. As the people demanded something besides manna to eat, Moses expressed himself in the most interesting of ways. He interpreted his situation in such a way that he believed God had surely forsaken him. Moses petitioned God: "Why have you dealt ill with your servant? And why have I not found favor in your sight, that you lay the burden of all this people on me? Did I conceive all this people? Did I give them birth, that you should say to me, 'Carry them in your bosom, as a nurse carries a nursing child,' to the land that you swore to give their fathers? . . . I am not able to carry all this people alone; the burden is too heavy for me. If you will treat me like this, kill me at once, if I find favor in your sight, that I may not see my wretchedness" (Num 11:11–16 ESV). The way Moses understood the trials of his work was the 'burden' of the people, under which he saw himself as ill-treated by God and better off dead. Precisely as he endured the turmoil commensurate with the servant vocation, he believed himself stricken by God; and yet, God was in fact using this battered soul for his purposes all the way along. Our account begs the question, "Are we to agree with Moses' reading of the situation, or God's?"

Scene 2

Jesus hung on a cross because he would not cease in praying "but your will be done." He hung on a cross because the scribes, Pharisees, and chief priests were serving god. He hung on a cross, and for that reason, everyone had sufficient reason to regard him a false and failed messiah. The excited dreams of tearless pastures were washed away by the flood of sorrow and demise.

A people so properly unfamiliar with Moses thought that this one who hung on a cross was forsaken by God, dying under the law in the name of justice. This would have been correct had Jesus not interjected, "Why are you weeping?" (John 20:15). For God *raised* this man! God raised *this man*! *God* raised this man![1] We were sure he was forsaken, stricken, afflicted by God.

He was, but his affliction was on account of God giving him the work of a servant and at the hands of the very people he came to save. Our petition "My God, my God, why have you forsaken me?" was on the lips of I AM. It was not God who had forsaken the world; it was the world that had forsaken God. He was "despised, and we esteemed him not. . . . His generation . . . considered that he was cut off out of the land of the living," and "they made his grave" (Isa 53:3, 8, 9 ESV). *Yet*, "surely he has borne our griefs, and carried our sorrows" and "upon him was the chastisement that brought us peace" (Isa 53:4–5). The power of life's great enemy was undone in the raising of Christ, for death had done its worst and had been found wanting. In Christ, we all might taste of love and life incorruptible: "Do you not know that all of us who have been baptized into Christ Jesus were baptized into his death? Therefore we have been buried with him by baptism into death, so that, just as Christ was raised from the dead by the glory of the Father, so we too might walk in newness of life" (Rom 6:2–4 ESV).

1. This is an explicit allusion to Barth's tripartite phraseology of revelation. Barth, *Church Dogmatics*, 1/1, 296.

Atonement

The resurrection is the reality which makes eternal life possible. As Moses cried out in the tone of a once enslaved Israel, remembering also Isaiah's servant who wore affliction to remedy his people's affliction, Jesus was regarded as forsaken that his people "shall no more be termed Forsaken" (Isa 62:4 ESV).

Jesus brought to our attention the conclusion of that Psalm: "O my God, I cry by day, but you do not answer, and by night, but I find no rest. Yet you are holy, enthroned on the praises of Israel. In you our fathers trusted; they trusted, and you delivered them . . . in you they trusted and were not put to shame. . . . You who fear the LORD, praise him! All you offspring of Jacob, glorify him, and stand in awe of him, all you offspring of Israel! For he has not despised or abhorred the affliction of the afflicted, and he has not hidden his face from him. . . . May your hearts live forever!" (Ps 22:2–3, 23–24, 26 ESV).

Epilogue

There is perhaps nothing more appropriate to say in response than "in him was life, and the life was the light of all people. The light shines in the darkness, and the darkness did not overcome it" (John 1:4–5).

God did not remain high upon the proverbial mountain, waiting upon humanity to "get themselves in order" that they might be pleasing in his sight; rather, the God on the mountain is now the one on the altar. At the summation of human efforts to appease a temperamental deity, the God who is thought to be pleased is pleased to lay his life down for his people. In fact, God does not love his people sacrificing to him for his glory, rather he is willing to be sacrificed for the love of his people, which is his glory (cf. Ps. 40:6). Israel's formative cultic practices have been preparing them for their face-to-face with God. And while humanity attempted to bring glory to the god on the Holy Hill, the King of Glory was beaten and battered behind the scenes. Whereby an estranged religious premise sought to prepare God for what he would see in humanity, now we see that it has always been God preparing humanity for what they would see in Jesus the Christ.

To give what is due to Jesus and what transpired in his death, we are obliged to name this atrocity, heinous, nefarious: a senseless and unspeakable evil. To give what is due to Jesus and the end to which he suffered, we are obliged to name this compassionate, kenotic, wise.

The fathers of the church were fond of seeing a single and decisive act of God in the cross that is both just and loving. In what way was the cross a victory over evil? With evil there is no distinction between its success and its obliteration. For it is parasitic and destructive to that which God has given life. Like a beast devouring without restrain to the point of sickness and death, this disease will not identify what is necessary for its own existence. For death's ravenous consumption of that very principle upon which the cosmos rests, namely the eternal Logos of God—Jesus of Nazareth, has sealed for eternity the fate of this evil age: it has been sealed with the crucified body of our Lord.

And yet, like the ark departing for a promised future, Christ was raised to newness. Moreover he invites the world to know him and be sealed, not in the body of the crucified, but in the resurrection. Death has no claim over the new domain and kingdom for which we hope. Like a fish hooked by the bait (Gregory of Nyssa), or a mouse snagged by a trap (Augustine), sin has tasted of both success and extinction. Gregory of Nyssa writes, "For from this approximation of death to life, of darkness to light, of corruption to incorruption, there is effected an obliteration of what is worse, and a passing away of it into nothing, while benefit is conferred on him who is freed from those evils."[2]

---

2. Gregory of Nyssa, *Catechism*, 26.

Atonement

[Praise be to] Christ Jesus, who, though he was in the form of God, did not count equality with God a thing to be grasped, but emptied himself, by taking the form of a servant, being born in the likeness of men. And being found in human form, he humbled himself by becoming obedient to the point of death, even death on a cross. Therefore God has highly exalted him and bestowed on him the name that is above every name, so that at the name of Jesus every knee should bow, in heaven and on earth and under the earth, and every tongue confess that Jesus Christ is Lord, to the glory of God the Father.

—PHILIPPIANS 2:5–11 ESV

5
Resurrection

But on the first day of the week, at early dawn, they went to the tomb, taking the spices they had prepared. And they found the stone rolled away from the tomb, but when they went in they did not find the body of the Lord Jesus. While they were perplexed about this, behold, two men stood by them in dazzling apparel. And as they were frightened and bowed their faces to the ground, the men said to them, "Why do you seek the living among the dead?"

—LUKE 24:1–5

God anointed Jesus of Nazareth with the Holy Spirit and with power. He went about doing good and healing all who were oppressed by the devil, for God was with him. And we are witnesses of all that he did both in the country of the Jews and in Jerusalem. They put him to death by hanging him on a tree, but God raised him on the third day.

—ACTS 10:38–40 ESV

If Christ has not been raised, your faith is futile and you are still in your sins.

—1 CORINTHIANS 15:17

Resurrection

FOR ALL THE DRAMATIC effect, the emotional jubilance, the mental unraveling of the resurrection, it is not uncommon that this fantastic event is deemed incidental. Whether that be because its miraculous nature is altogether troubling or it is regarded as a mere affirmation—a telling once and for of the Son's glory, Paul's absolutizing insistence upon it never ceases to find a surprised audience.

On the Road

Venturing toward a village named "Emmaus" outside of Jerusalem, two of Jesus' disciples were reflecting upon recent events. Bewildered, confused, wanting, they try for resolve and find only that hollowed and painful anxiety which accompanies disaster: "We had hoped that he was the one to redeem Israel" (Luke 24:21).

Our truest being, as those for whom infinite longing and love is our stay, is only viable in hope. For it tells of that existence which neither time nor nature diminishes; hope is the premise of our being. And, how swiftly do the winds of sorrow invade a hopeless existence. For we may be filled with wine, laughter, and pleasure, great works—in houses and vineyards, gardens and parks; we may have servants, spouses, singers, and lovers, but confess: "Whatever my eyes desired I did not keep from them; I kept my heart from no pleasure, for my heart found pleasure in all my toil, and this was my reward for all my toil. Then I considered all that my hands had done and the toil I had spent in doing it, and again, all was vanity and a chasing after wind, and there was nothing to be gained under the sun" (Eccl 2:10–11).

Nevertheless, the two disciples proceed with business, bearing up under the new weight of vanity that has come their way, "looking sad" (Luke 24:17). And yet we are reminded of the Apostle Paul's words regarding hope. For he reminds us that while knowledge and prophecy face a definite "end," perceiving only through a dimly lit mirror in a "childish" and "partial" way, hope is among those few things that transcend our lot in a shifting and uncertain world (1 Cor 13:8–13). Hope stands in continuity with that "complete" image, when we see "face to face" (1 Cor 13:10, 12).

In a scene which causes us to well up with emotion, Jesus "came near" unannounced and their eyes were "kept from recognizing him" (Luke 24:15–16). And with near frustrating nonchalance Jesus asks them about the conversation they were having as they walked along the road. With justifiably abrasive tone, one named Cleopas retorted, "Are you the only stranger in Jerusalem who does not know the things that have taken place?" (Luke 24:18). However, it is the hopeless who are plagued with a certain blindness. For they regarded the testimony of the women at the tomb as an "idle tale" (Luke 24:11) and were unable to see before their faces the Son in Glory. Therefore Jesus responded with rebuke, "Oh, how foolish you are, and how slow of heart to believe" (Luke 24:25). Taking them to Moses and the prophets, Jesus interpreted the whole of Scripture in light of himself and the necessity of his suffering (Luke 24:27).

And as they approached the village Jesus gestured as if he intended to continue further still, at which point the disciples compelled him to stay and join them for the evening. Therefore, "when he was at table with them, he took the bread and blessed and broke it and gave it to them. And their eyes were opened" (Luke 24:30–31 ESV).

A home frail and derided is illumined *at table* by the enchanting nearness of Christ; an occasioning proper to understanding alone, for "he is not far from each one of us. For 'In him we live and move and have our being'" (Acts 17:27–28). Jesus had been among them all along, the truth of his life and testimony exuding victory and validity yet unconsidered by the hopeless. The eerie spaciousness of Christ's interaction with the two on the road invites us to regard the magnitude. The elongated silence and indirect inquiries, while unbecoming in the immediate context, envision the universality of the event. For what would be shared among the three on their way to Emmaus was the debut of history's grandest reveal, life's enigmatic crescendo. For what domain of existence remains unaffected by this event? What consideration deemed irrelevant?

Fundamentally, Jesus was not a liar. He *is* the Son, the *monogenes*, of the Father. He was in and of the Spirit of God, "knowing"

Resurrection

God—sharing, experiencing, possessing. Jesus was always the gift and grace of the Spirit, his delight. When no one has seen God, he has; and by seeing *him* we see YHWH. We witness in the resurrection a new *toledoth*, a new generation, for the sons and daughters of heaven. We learn that God is faced with no opposite or polarity and has decided power over Sheol. We learn that Job's sinless tribulation is realized in Christ, and thereby his condemnation was not consequent of sin or failing. Therefore, Jesus' life was of love; and because he told us to see in his life very God of very God, we know that God is love. We know the congregation of the Lord owns an inheritance of sublime nature, a land flowing with the incomparable. We learn that the tyrant is a liar, and the meek mock the proud by their graciousness. All in all, we learn that our nature was never to remain *under the sun*. Hope knows all things, endures all things. In this way, the *table* is given to the world as eyes to see and ears to hear, that in all things it might "recognize him."

Signs of Things to Come

As event the resurrection is a telling of the end. Moreover, the resurrection is proleptic; for not only does it *tell* of the end but *is* the end. The resurrection is not a prophetic demonstration like that of the old charismatic and flagrant figures of Israel, nor is it a foreshadowing embodied in physical manifestation. The exact conclusion of history *took place* in the definite event of Jesus Christ.

Evinced in the Apostle Paul, endurance and anticipation are directed toward the end, our end, in the risen Christ. Though "suffering the loss of all things," the apostle considers them "rubbish" (Phil 3:8), and the suffering that is owed to his faithfulness to Christ is not reason for concern—whether that be lamenting unto a God who is slow to act, questioning his own spiritual state, or doubting God's loving-kindness. For, all that he endures is no longer the powerless and isolated destitution of one abandoned, rather his tribulation has become "the sharing of *his* sufferings" (Phil 3:10).

Behold Our God

There is a mysterious union. In the "knowing" of Christ Jesus, our suffering no longer resides in the collateral damage of life's savagery but owns a "share" *in Christ*—we being present in his passion, and his passion being present in us. And as the first fruit of a new creation, Christ embarks toward heaven's call, and those *knowing*—or sharing in—him know also the "power of his resurrection" (Phil 3:10). The lucid mystical exchange of passion is transposed throughout his works. The finitude of our corporeal existence finds itself not in a fullness acquired by its own accomplishment, it is not "good" or "satisfied" at once, but in the act of transcending itself it truly becomes itself; it does not lose its particularity, but "becomes" in the traversal of the infinite—the ever outward motion of the soul. Therefore, our suffering is no longer "ours" but a *sharing* in Christ's, likewise our death and resurrection are not isolated occurrences but the provision of unity with the risen Christ. Our virtue is not a fulfilling of our creatureliness, rather our creatureliness is fulfilled in sharing the virtue of another. We do not possess a "righteousness" of our own, but the "righteousness [of] God" (Phil 3:9).

This unity precludes us from making an end of the creature, as those for whom "their god is the belly" with minds "set on earthly things" (Phil 3:19). For "our citizenship is in heaven," and "he will transform the body of our humiliation that it may be conformed to the body of his glory" (Phil 3:20, 21).

In this way, Christ sums up, or more precisely *"recapitulates,"* all things. Just as all commandments emanate from and return to "love," in that they are "recapitulated" (*anakephalaioo*) by love (Rom 13:9), so too is everything taken up by its head, Christ Jesus. For all things, things in heaven and on earth, are "recapitulated" in Christ (Eph 1:10): as Paul says: "He is the image of the invisible God, the firstborn of all creation.... He himself is before all things, and in him all things hold together. He is the head of the body, the church; he is the beginning, the firstborn from the dead, so that he might come to have first place in everything. For in him all the fullness of God was pleased to dwell, and through him God was pleased to reconcile to himself all things" (Col 1:15, 17–20).

By drawing up the human being through his being human, the God-man is at work, though not the work of an independent connoisseur of the human race, but as the grace and form of humanity. Christ as the original utterance, the archetypal image according to which the human person is intelligible, is exposited along the sacred themes of the infinite. He proceeds from the Father as the differentiation and beloved of the Father while reciprocating in a divine instance, constituting the nature of fatherhood. As the icon, Christ is celebrated and embraced by the Spirit, the love of God. And therefore Athanasius could say, "He was made man that we might be made God."[1] The elusive "image" that had only provisionally inspired humanity was revealed in the incarnate Logos:

> The Jews answered, "It is not for a good work that we are going to stone you, but for blasphemy, because you, though only a human being, are making yourself God." Jesus answered, "Is it not written in your law, 'I said, you are gods'? ... Those to whom the word of God came were called 'gods.'" (John 10:33–35)

Preparing Meals with Lazarus

As genuinely spectacular as this theme is, the glorified existence of resurrected life, there is a halting qualification. For while the power of God is at work in us—moving us along in righteousness—we can only claim to know the *taste* of the resurrection. The good gifts of the divine life do not circumvent our *place* in the order of salvation. That place is our "being reconciled," the ongoingness of the process itself. We know, therefore, temporality as ones mingling in a time between times. The contrasting and striking images of being crucified and made alive represent subsequent realities at work throughout the course of our life, appropriately understood as "renewal" or more precisely "transformation" (Rom 12:2). Those impediments that war with the new nature appear under the guise of liberty only to idolize pleasure—an erroneous

---

1. Athanasius, *On the Incarnation*, 66.

and decayed portrayal of the beautiful; and therefore they obstruct the *freedom* of being according to Being.

That freedom is the result of God's love, the outworking of his being "for us" from the beginning. For the same Jesus who wept alongside the tomb of Lazarus, passerbyers saying "See how he loved" (John 11:36), is sanctified by the Father for his ways and will for the world. As ones likened unto Lazarus, one whom Jesus *loved* (John 11:3), we were overcome by the abiding slumber of spiritual darkness. But those in darkness have seen a great light, for we are of those who have heard the command, "come out" (John 11:43). And once out we may be deceived by the miraculous, distracted by the attention of the crowds, and awestruck by the vision of Jesus Christ before us. For it is only days before Lazarus will have to prepare a meal for Jesus and company. A table requires setting; meal preparation need be underway with proportionate amounts of food and drink. Places will need arranging.

As the meal is underway, we see in Mary and Martha the tension between having the Son of God in their midst (John 12:8; cf. Luke 10:38–42) and having to look after the more mundane realities of everyday life. Moreover, an argument ensues over Mary's behavior, that of pouring ointment over Jesus' feet (John 12:3–5). And as all of this is going on, Lazarus reclines among them no doubt lacking in focus, attempting to catch up with reality as he reflects on the recent incident of his rising from the dead. It would seem a rather strange thing to be arguing over perfume having been raised from a tomb within days. And yet here he is, with tomorrow to deal with.

It is this very quirky, and at times troubling, way about life that characterizes our place: sublime and rapturous at one moment, tedious and ordinary at another. We conduct ourselves out of the narrative of "the resurrection and the life" (John 11:25), and yet feel contradicted by the remorseless pace of everyday.

However, in that confused state Lazarus drew people to Christ: "On account of him . . . many of the Jews were deserting and were believing in Jesus" (John 12:11). Something of God's nature was portrayed in and through this risen one, and *through* him the light of life spread into the world, for "the world has gone after him" (John 12:19). And as the news of Jesus' miracle spread they noticed that even the Greeks had come to see him, news that communicated the grandeur of Jesus' stage.

He declared that the time had come for him to be "lifted up from the earth" that he might "draw all people" (John 12:32): a moment "for the Son of Man to be glorified" (John 12:23), and at once a glorifying of the Father (John 12:28). Forever after, this moment will be the enigmatic "*in this way*" of God's love (John 3:16), the *way* that gestures the mind of God and his will in Christ—that which speaks forth the love and light of the divine. And *in this way*, God is glorified. Therefore the cross and resurrection share in the same revelatory act by which God is made known. There is something so properly Christian about an uncomfortably earthly existence.

The resurrection is thus a principle. As Jesus says, "Whoever serves me must follow me, and where I am, there will my servant be also" (John 12:26). We are those who are found in Christ's "way," that twofold path of cross and resurrection, which is communicative of his grace poured out for the world. We suffer illness leading not to death but for "God's glory, so that the Son of God may be glorified through it" (John 11:4). Therefore, this time between times takes on the form of vocation. For what else should we pray, "Father, save me from this hour"? Rather, it is the time in which we extend the love of God in and through the ways of God.

Behold Our God

> Baptism into the death and resurrection of Christ then means that the goal of redemption is already attained, for in this baptism eternity is sacramentally present. The believing participant is transposed from the realm of death, of constraining forces and of the old aeon of transience into the eternally present realm of freedom, of heavenly life and of resurrection. All that now remains for him on earth is to exhibit his new, heavenly nature in freedom. In the sacramental and spiritual presence of Christ, resurrection from the dead is already imparted to the receivers and is eternally present to them. The earthly body and the things of the world fade away to become for them an unreal semblance, in the disregarding of which they must give proof of their heavenly freedom.

—JÜRGEN MOLTMANN[2]

---

2. *Theology of Hope*, 155–56.

6
Word

In the beginning was the Word, and the Word was with God, and the Word was God. He was in the beginning with God. All things came into being through him, and without him not one thing came into being.
—JOHN 1:1–3

The word of God is living and active, sharper than any two-edged sword, piercing until it divides soul from spirit, joints from marrow; it is able to judge the thoughts and intentions of the heart. And before him no creature is hidden, but all are naked and laid bare to the eyes of the one to whom we must render an account.
—HEBREWS 4:12–13

THAT WE CAN TALK about divine speech is a luxury; that we can witness God's Word is cataclysmic. Given the variety of ways in which the phrase "word" applies we will consider the follow delineations on the theme: Logos, Revelation, Witness.

Logos

In the furry of opening sequences found in the Gospel of Mark, ever propelled by his signature phrase "immediately," Jesus does nothing less than burst onto the messianic scene. The account is overflowing with stories that exude Jesus' uniqueness; however, this is not a uniqueness due a prophet, sage, or ruler who is distinguished in their era, rather Jesus is distinguished in a novel fashion.

At "the beginning of the good news," people from various regions were flocking to the wilderness to hear a man name John the Baptizer (Mark 1:1). He knew not the comfort of a nobleman but the plight of a prophet, eating locusts and honey while clothed by the hide of a camel. And winning no one over by charm, he was appointed to usher Christ out into the world, and proclaimed a baptism of repentance: a messenger sent ahead to "prepare the way" (Mark 1:3).

And to his horror, the very one who occupied his preaching came to be baptized. However, the moment that Christ proceeded forth from the waters, the heavens were torn apart and "the Spirit descended like a dove on him" (Mark 1:10). The prophetic climax of John's preparatory vocation culminated from his hands through the waters to heaven itself as history beckoned that most blessed arrival of the only begotten Son: "You are my Son, the Beloved; with you I am well pleased" (Mark 1:11).

What God revealed in the baptism of Christ would unfold in the subsequent encounters that were to follow. Christ's work throughout his ministry was not intended to accomplish particular acts, but in those acts display the nature of God. And it is through the displaying that he woos the world for himself.

Christ sees in his acts the outworkings of the "kingdom of God" which he proclaimed was at hand, the time being "fulfilled" (Mark 1:15). His life has a sort of grammar that communicates something of his nature in and through his works. For this is God's chosen one, seen before time and sought throughout history. Being driven into the wilderness to surmount temptation for forty days (Mark 1:12), designating a new group of twelve around himself

(Mark 1:16–20), and silencing the confession of an unclean spirit ("I know who you are, the Holy One of God" [Mark 1:24]), Christ takes up into himself the basic history of Israel itself. And yet, his fulfillment of history is accompanied by a speech that iterates his divinity, forgiving sins and calling God "father."

In this way, Jesus dramatizes the essence of God as a revelatory unfolding of the divine logic. Thus, as eternal Logos he *was* and *was with* God (John 1:1). The incarnate Word is the purposive self-revelation of God, the defining appearance of his most intimate being. The incarnation is the dawn of "that which I am" from the "I am" (cf. Exod 3:14). Ever blessed is the divine Son who is beheld by the Father and embraced in the Spirit, the Son receiving sonship and returning fatherhood. Each member of the Trinity exists for and in the other, and only thus are they known. Therefore the Logos is the logic and truth of Being. The inauguration of the kingdom is none other than the bringing to bear all things in Christ. Reality then can be said to be christologically shaped, understanding that God's existence *is* his triune essence and creation simply participates in *his* existence. God's acts of justice and mercy are an extension of his own harmony, instantiations of the sacred and infinite Sabbath.

Revelation

That we can learn of Christ's life and deduce historical, theological, and philosophical realities is a convenience of his coming into the world. While the incarnate Christ is the definitive self-revelation of God, "revelation" as a concept has another reference. It is a category which delineates the phenomenon of God's appearing to us. His appearing is not limited to a specific medium nor necessitated by a particular practice. It is original to God and comes from beyond ourselves. And what is crucial to distinguish is that this phenomenon refers not merely to a collection of data—a depository of invaluable facts as it were—but simply *that* God has emerged in an appearance worthy of "revelation."

Because of its supernatural character it eludes easy articulation, and because it is difficult to reduce and simplify as an idea we are in danger of misleading ourselves, should we employ inappropriate descriptions. For we are tempted in the light of such phrases as "appearing" and "revealing" to envision action. However, we would be remiss to conceive of divine action in a way that implied a kind of gulf between what would be God's removed dwelling and our desolate estate. Therefore, whatever we say of the appearing of God must always consider his transcendence and simplicity; God is so thoroughly beyond that he repels distinctions between present and absent, removed and near.

Furthermore, because God is simple—that is, all that God is he is at once—his consciousness is not bound to a definite perspective but is comprehensively determinative for all consciousness as such—as the original and formal vista of rationality. Therefore, we would be negligent to speak of revelation in a way that implies God's attention is somehow elsewhere prior to intervening in our lives. God is "an act of infinite knowledge" and "the absolute unity of consciousness and being."[1]

Therefore when we speak about God's appearing, we are to avoid language of activity that would betray fundamental Christian convictions about God's nature. But when that moment comes, when God becomes God *to us*, it is characteristic of a movement on God's part yet striking as an awareness of what has always been. Revelation is that startling apprehension of the consciousness which has always beheld us. It is one thing to discover an objective fact that has only subtly escaped our notice, but quite another for that fact to be comprehending, knowledgeable, and alive.

As an appearing, revelation composes its own event in the fluidity of life's moments. Even in prayer and liturgical living, one still feels the changeable tide of its coming and going. And in the attempt to conjure it, we are taught of its unbounded nature as nothing can reliably contain or package the innocence of apprehension. Yet this category, this conceptual sphere, of revelation is demonstrative of our relation toward God on the whole. We are

---

1. Hart, *Experience of God*, 235.

Word

at all times invited in his embrace having confidence in his imminence and reverence toward his freedom. And this event instills the absolute completeness of God who is our desire and can be replaced by no finite end.

However, what also accompanies this advent is the impending affront on our being. Nothing so clarifies the emptiness of our form, the ignorance of our vision, and the vanity of our virtue. Revelation is condemning in the sense that it situates humanity in its frailty and crystalizes God's supremacy in all and through all. It is as if being cradled we were swooped downward, feeling our center quickly drawn away from us. One cannot derail its effect by turning a blind eye or reframing it in their favor, for revelation is God's appearance *with* its own interpretation. We do not have life in ourselves. And what is more, our transgressions have been against the one who is life and gives life, the one who now confronts us.

Thus it is precisely the word of the gospel that meets us in the confrontation with the infinite and gives that timeless decree of love. What we may have read in Scripture or heard from preaching comes to life as if for the very first time. He reminds us of his word, and his word forever determines the shape of his appearing.

Witness

We see in the testimony of the gospels those treasured narratives of Christ. However, they will remain nothing more than narratives so long as the God of Jesus Christ does not speak these realities to us in the present. We might ask ourselves, how is it that Christ himself could appear and yet some of his contemporaries lack the proper fear and trembling owed to the revealing of God? How is it that Nicodemus could call Jesus the teacher from God, and yet be blind and dead toward God's kingdom? How is it that Paul should refer to God's truth as foolishness and folly (1 Cor 1:18–31)? Why does the preached word, not to mention the incarnate Word, fail to have consistent effect? What is true of this message—or what is proper to this gospel—is that rote repetition can never replace the divine utterance of God's self-revelation.

There is an incomparable distinction between hearing Jesus imply his divinity and being confronted by God in Christ. There is a distinction between reading inscribed texts and having God beckon you through his Word. By what means do we call Scripture God's word? Whatever response we shall give will merely supplement the simple fact that it knows us: he knows us. Therefore we find ourselves saying something like, "He revealed himself to me." We are entirely incapable of replicating it, and therefore can only bear witness to it: the Word of God is alive. It has "pierced" our very souls (Heb 4:12).

This emphasis of the Word of God *confronting* us in the present, is an important one. It is no doubt true that Scripture contains a written witness borne of the Holy Spirit, and therefore tending to the texts themselves is entailed in remaining faithful to the tradition passed from Jesus through the apostles. But within that tradition, and what we find recorded in the witness of Scripture itself, is not the idea that these texts can replace an authentically divine utterance in the present (this is not the divine utterance of an essentially new message, rather it is the divine address to the hearer *through* the classic Christian gospel). In fact, we see a looking forward *in* the proclamation of the word to the God who speaks in a way that only he can. When the Apostle Paul describes the way he preached the gospel, he said that his speech was intentionally humble in nature in order to lead the hears' attention to the powerfully spoken Word that comes from God: "My speech and my proclamation were not with plausible words of wisdom, but with a demonstration of the Spirit and of power, so that your faith might rest not on human wisdom but on the power of God" (1 Cor 2:4–5). Even the inspired preaching of the apostle which would contribute to the formation of sacred text is seen "in weakness and in fear and in much trembling" (v. 3). To put it another way, the reading of Scripture alone cannot demand upon the movement of God as a diviner's incantation. Therefore, the reading, preaching, and praying of Scripture must be done with the reverence suitable

Word

to the God who freely comes and goes like the wind—a wind which all too easily escapes our attempt to control it (John 3:8).

Thus when we read in the life of Jesus, in the preaching of the apostles, and the testimony of scriptural epistles that the proclamation of the word was done in fear, it is neither incidental nor complimentary. The actual *content* of those witness *is* the pointing gesture of those who are recipients of Revelation, the Word of God. Revelation therefore is an event that formally speaking cannot be contained by any preaching, and in this way the apostolic tradition understood its role as *witnessing* and giving *testimony*. It is for these reasons that the one who crept unannounced to Jesus while it was dark would be found in the day receiving Jesus' body from the cross: "Joseph of Arimathea, who was a disciple of Jesus, though a secret one because of his fear of the Jews, asked Pilate to let him take away the body of Jesus. Pilate gave him permission; so he came and removed his body. Nicodemus, who had at first come to Jesus by night, also came" (John 19:38–39; cf. John 3:1). We are those who once approached by night and now wait with bated breath at his glorious appearing in and through his testimonies, a revelation veiled by the folly and scandal of its form—though we are those who tenderly receive it from its shame.

For as the aged, or those whose sight is defective, when any book, however fair, is set before them, though they perceive that there is something written, are scarcely able to make out two consecutive words, but, when aided by glasses, begin to read distinctly, so Scripture, gathering together the impressions of Deity, which, till then, lay confused in their minds, dissipates the darkness, and shows us the true God clearly. God therefore bestows a gift of singular value, when, for the instruction of the Church, he employs not dumb teachers merely, but opens his own sacred mouth; when he not only proclaims that some God must be worshipped, but at the same time declares that He is the God to whom worship is due.

—JOHN CALVIN[2]

2. *Institutes*, 1.6.1.

7
Sacrament

"This Is My Body"

So Jesus said to them, "Very truly, I tell you, unless you eat the flesh of the Son of Man and drink his blood, you have no life in you. Those who eat my flesh and drink my blood have eternal life, and I will raise them up on the last day; for my flesh is true food and my blood is true drink. Those who eat my flesh and drink my blood abide in me, and I in them. Just as the living Father sent me, and I live because of the Father, so whoever eats me will live because of me. This is the bread that came down from heaven, not like that which your ancestors ate, and they died. But the one who eats this bread will live forever."

—JOHN 6:53–58

For as often as you eat this bread and drink the cup, you proclaim the Lord's death until he comes.

—1 COR 11:26

THE TERM "PROCLAMATION" APPEARS to fit most naturally with a verbal message to proclaim, we are in no shortage of Christian material that would pair "word" with "proclamation." And yet this term invites a far richer consideration. Indeed, we would be remiss

Sacrament

to consider such a word as primarily regarding information, that which is to be stated once and for all.

We need reminding, exhorting, admonishing: "Therefore I intend to keep on reminding you of these things, though you know them already and are established in the truth that has come to you. I think it right, as long as I am in this body, to refresh your memory" (2 Pet 1:12–13). In fact it would be a misguided idea to think we carry on with our lives simply needing the correct message to orient that life. In observing our nature, things actually look very different than this. We do not carry on with our lives as distinct from the hearing of the Word of God; rather we *are*—our lives *are*—a hearing of the Word, a ceaseless and reverent posture toward God, ever recipients. By way of extension, it makes a great deal of sense that the Lord would give a tangible expression of this fact, which would be constitutive for the Christian's very being; for we are brought now to the thing called "Communion," "Eucharist," "The Lord's Supper," all of which point to the church's being *at table* (cf. Luke 22:14).

Just as the apostles were "given" the gospel, the inexplicable power of God (Rom 1:16), to proclaim to the world, so too were they given the gift of the table. The Apostle Paul says, "For I received from the Lord what I also handed on to you, that the Lord Jesus on the night when he was betrayed took a loaf of bread" (1 Cor 11:23). This tradition is presented more thoroughly in the gospel accounts as that which came from the hand of the Lord Jesus.

The fellowship, vulnerability, and nourishment that are true of all tables are neither accidental nor conveniently metaphorical. For it is precisely in the doing of the table that we know the fellowship, vulnerability, and nourishment of Christ. As a remembering of his life, an enactment of his presence, and an anticipation of his coming, the supper defines our past, present, and future. Jesus said, "For I tell you, I will not eat it [again] until it is fulfilled in the kingdom of God . . . I will not drink of the fruit of the vine until the kingdom of God comes" (Luke 22:16, 18). The Apostle Paul suggests that in this observance we "proclaim the Lord's death until he comes" (1 Cor 11:26). Thus it is in the church's receiving that it proclaims.

When Paul critiqued the Corinthian community for the self-seeking manner in which they reclined at the table, he suggested that in doing so they became "guilty concerning the body and blood of the Lord" (1 Cor 11:27 ESV). The bread is linked directly with Christ, his bodily nearness is mediated through the body of the bread. Therefore, our behavior toward the table is our behavior toward Christ. The church's existence is the supper, for it can only be the "body of Christ" in so far as it shares in the table: "The bread that we break, is it not a participation in the body of Christ?" (1 Cor 10:16 ESV).

The Elements

That being said, should we suppose such non-miraculous content as simple bread and wine be the constituting substance of our being? This question is a fair one; it is a historically contentious one. These elements have been metaphysically dubious. Throughout the course of debate, the concern has been to discern the qualitative variable responsible for the vast spiritual implications of the elements: what is unique about *this* bread and wine? And yet, to dwell on the material content of the elements may be misleading.

Confronted by the very ordinary nature of these elements, the observer may have two reactions: one may deem erroneous the participatory theology (or, sacramental ontology), and insist that the elements are symbolic; or affirm the ontological relationship and conclude that the elements must be of greater spiritual content than meets the eye. However, it is unhelpful to allow this polarity to misrepresent either the transcendent or particular qualities.

The uncontained nature of God's Being so appropriately graces our lives in ways tangible yet sublime, penetrating though disentangled. Therefore the unsolicited play between form and content so properly depicts the contingency of our lives. We are faithful in attending though powerless in our receiving. The table is a sacred instantiation of what we are, a locus of demonstration and observation. Jesus' word was difficult for some and life-giving

Sacrament

for others; so in *beholding* the table as Christ's table, it becomes life-giving because he becomes life-giving. And by coming to receive we receive from Christ.

Therefore, as it is with the proclamation of the Word, the supper is the presence of that which not only shapes our being but is our being. Communion is formative; but it is more. We are not creatures who practice a thing called Communion; we *are* attendees at the table, through which we find our being as creatures. In this way, the indivisible unity of "body" finds the church dependent upon an earthen vessel as is appropriate from a truly earthen God-man.

Baptizing Them in the Name

Before many of us know the table firsthand, we pass through a divine initiation: baptism. In its simplest explanation, baptism accompanies, testifies, and mediates one's joining "in Christ" through faith(fulness). It is not coerced; it is a choice—regardless of the ecclesial mode one takes. Yet as a choice, it is also the passive recognition of the truth—an act which is not obviously synonymous with "choice." We might diffuse this tension by appealing to "faith"; however, this brings forth an interesting question: how is this moment of baptism, representative of one's initiation into the life of God, equally that of choice on the one hand and passive recognition on the other? Surely "faith" is not virtuous in and of itself, divorced from the appropriate context for that faith.

The two are held together by the condition of courage. The instant of baptism is nothing less than courageous because in full light of the truth that lies ahead the baptized actually makes a decision leading unto death. All that was is now "in Christ." For whosoever might save their life, will surely lose it (Mark 8:35); "Foxes have holes, and birds of the air have nests; but the Son of Man has nowhere to lay his head" (Luke 9:58–59). And what is more, "no one who puts a hand to the plow and looks back is fit for the kingdom of God" (v. 62). To see and to step forward in faith(fulness) is to behold the cross of Jesus Christ—in everything that it is—and look down beside oneself only to find lying there a second cross, waiting to be carried.

And yet, is this just another occasion for scoffers, critics, and the like to paint a picture of a uniquely cruel and devious god who takes great delight in the ascetic torments of those he would not otherwise call followers? Even if we should not fall victim to such depictions, surely we do not escape even a straightforward reading of these texts without the grimace which accompanies admonitions unto death. Perhaps those accustomed to that certain preaching of the word which makes consistent use of the kingdom-world (spirit-flesh) dichotomy will receive such instruction with a subconsciously arrogant posture toward "dying to self." Whatever the case may be, a practice which signifies, celebrates, and mediates one's own death is just peculiar enough to warrant considerable attention and reflection. How then ought we to rightly think about dying in an appropriate manner?

Our thinking must quickly relate the extremities of the previous motif, that is bearing one's own cross through baptism, with the words of our Lord who said:

> Come to me, all who labor and are heavy laden, and I will give you rest. Take my yoke upon you, and learn from me, for I am gentle and lowly in heart, and you will find rest for your souls. For my yoke is easy, and my burden is light. (Matt 11:28–30 ESV)

We can think of few heavier "yokes"; and yet, we somehow take this to be true. While much careless speech has attributed to God the role of comforter, counselor, and everlasting provider, that is to say superfluous recognition of God's provision borne out of verbal practices alone, those people who so *remain* in God continue to know the peace that is true of his being. It is a curious fact that the people of God have ceaselessly abided by these words, "Prince of Peace," and thereby have been so nourished in spirit that they say "In God alone is my delight." That being said, there may be hesitation from those of a privileged position to so candidly call God "our peace" while reaping the harvest of other's labor: this cannot be justified away, as it were. But what needs be said is this: it is of no

Sacrament

greater praise to be immersed in privilege and forever determining oneself unworthy of contentment. Contentment is not having little and learning to repudiate desire for greater things; rather, it is the capacity to peer through the veil of this world to the splendor of God.

There is no clearer and more penetrating description of this phenomenon than Jesus' account of the discovered treasure. "The kingdom of heaven is like treasure hidden in a field, which someone found and hid; then in his joy he goes and sells all that he has and buys that field" (Matt 13:44): a story quaint and succinct. What is so gripping about this parable is that we can indwell this individual and vicariously experience the joyous and bursting emotions of one who has stumbled upon a treasure of invaluable worth; it is too familiar a fantasy. It makes a great deal of sense that in finding such a treasure one could scamper off with satisfaction while brainstorming all the ways in which they could sell off their possessions. With each sale, each departure, this person swells with anticipation and excitement, as they become closer to obtaining the apple of their eye.

This leads us to consider Jesus' suggestion that whosoever would lose their life in this world will find life eternal. The celebration of baptism, therefore, is the joyous selling of all our "possessions" in the exuberant disposition of one who has found a great treasure. We are buried in Christ to the end of being raised with Christ.

We extol God who has drawn us up from the pit, out of the "miry bog," and set our feet upon—not shaky, insecure, or unstable foundations, but—*solid* ground. Standing upon a rock, we pronounce a new, and ever new, song through which God shall be praised; may many see, fear, and trust: for he is dazzling in his manifest worthiness (cf. Ps. 40:2–5). Therefore we exclaim, "I have told the glad news of deliverance in the great congregation; see, I have not restrained my lips, as you know, O LORD. I have not hidden your saving help within my heart, I have spoken of your faithfulness and your salvation; I have not concealed your steadfast love and your faithfulness from the great congregation" (Ps 40:9–10).

Woe Is Me

The light of this salvific spectacle is muted, even if temporarily, by that realization penetrating the soul: should God look toward me, after having redeemed the whole world, and name me precious—a "treasured possession" (cf. Deut 7:6; Ps 116:15; 1 Pet 2:9)? For reasons which may be obvious for some, it is an altogether more difficult and trying enterprise to know God's promises *as they relate to me*; this is hopefully not overwhelmingly cliché that its severity and reality do not lack the recognition warranted. Affirming the divine compassion secured for a friend is a ministry and service that can flow gracefully and with great delight, while taking hold of such things for one's self can be a fumbling uncertainty plagued by insecurity and self-doubt.

Perhaps God's forgiveness could not extend to the things I have done, or what if I have run up all my chances to repent? How might God's silence be a match for the unrestrained and grotesque thoughts which occupy my mind? Maybe I simply have not merited his attention. Such anxieties are in some way expected for the Christian. They are not predictable because everyone assuredly carries around hidden and heavy burdens. They are expected to the degree that we are in fact wanting creatures, and God is properly *awe*some. These fears are owed to a relationship with the truth. The "good news" of the gospel is not merely on account of one having a specific sin overbearing their life, rather this precious proclamation is so satisfying precisely because in the beholding of God there is always the arresting and condemning brilliance of his absolute purity and grandeur. It is a purifying judgment, refining those who would remain in him.

And even though we are but vapor subject to the wind likened unto a bruised reed and a frail leaf that has turned in color, our God has planted us by streams of water: living water which flows from the temple that is Jesus Christ, a river of life awakened by the Spirit of God. He has called us out from darkness, and nothing can separate us from his steadfast love and kindness. This did

Sacrament

not have to be, it does not have to be, but it is. And thus rightly we see our weakness as witness to his glory.

It is not the lone soul, the introspective, who is responsible for carrying the weight of knowing, securing, and embodying these promises. It is the nation of priests who uphold one another by the declaration of God's Word. How much sweeter is the nourishment of a word from a fellowship than a thought alone. What is more, this word-speaking, this proclamation, is not limited to the material interaction between persons, though of course this is an integral and vital component; rather this proclamation *is* who we *are*. Our identity, not being that of individuals who receive divine maintenance through timely words, is one always in motion toward God's proclivity "for us." That identity is shaped not *by* but *as* table fellowship. Therefore as table fellowship, we are a people stirred and reminded by God's Word to his church which is appropriated sacramentally. By the hands of fellow brothers and sisters we are recipients of God's nourishment: a receiving that transcends any single moment to determine the nature of the church. The receptive orientation of our Christian identity—as those *at table*—is more proper than who "I" am independent of my receiving from the fellowship.

This is what the talk about God that is to be found in the Church seeks to be when it is meant to be proclamation and is thus directed to men with the claim and expectation that it has to declare to them the Word of God. It can and should aim to be proclamation as preaching and sacrament because the Church has a commission to make such proclamation . . . we learn from the biblical witness to revelation that Jesus Christ has given His Church not only the commandment of faith and love and hope, nor merely the commandment to call upon His name in concert and to show brotherly love, etc., but also the commission of proclamation, and indeed of proclamation by preaching and sacrament.

—KARL BARTH[1]

1. *Church Dogmatics* 1/1, 56–57.

8
Church

He is the image of the invisible God, the firstborn of all creation. For by him all things were created, in heaven and on earth, visible and invisible, whether thrones or dominions or rulers or authorities—all things were created through him and for him. And he is before all things, and in him all things hold together. And he is the head of the body, the church. He is the beginning, the firstborn from the dead, that in everything he might be preeminent. For in him all the fullness of God was pleased to dwell, and through him to reconcile to himself all things, whether on earth or in heaven, making peace by the blood of his cross.

—COLOSSIANS 1:15–20

The church of God . . . those who are sanctified in Christ Jesus, called to be saints, together with all those who in every place call on the name of our Lord Jesus Christ, both their Lord and ours.

—1 CORINTHIANS 1:2

Though I am the very least of all the saints, this grace was given, to preach to the Gentiles the unsearchable riches of Christ, and to bring to light for everyone what is the plan of the mystery hidden for ages in God who created all things, so that through the church the manifold

Church

wisdom of God might now be made known to the rulers and authorities in the heavenly places. This was according to the eternal purpose that he has realized in Christ Jesus our Lord.

—EPHESIANS 3:8-11 ESV

What "Is" the Church?

IN TURNING ATTENTION TO considerations of the church, one is bombarded with a flood of images, ideas, experiences, sentiments, and the like; it is as though there are as many essences of what the church *is* as there are those willing to comment. As Lewis's Screwtape says to his minion Wormwood: "All your patient sees is the half-finished, sham Gothic erection on the new building estate."[1] There is no shortage of people, fiery and persuaded to the highest degree, seeking to implement what ought to be the case. More often than not, these versions of the church are inseparable from the social impulses out of which they emerged. And, in those instances when a genuinely Christian quality is reserved, there can follow an unfortunate imbalance in emphasis. While our view of the church may take a variety of shapes, we nevertheless all *see* the church *as* something—whether a "sham Gothic erection" or another.

There is perhaps no more striking and poignant way to put the matter than this: "Christian [fellowship] is not an ideal which we must realize; it is rather a reality created by God in Christ in which we may participate."[2] "Church" names those people who are, to their delight, encompassed in the life of God; they hallow the Father in the Spirit according to the Son, and thereby behold God. While it is tempting to turn to those practical realities which *characterize* the church—such as preaching, service, and evangelism for instance—we must be weary of the pitfalls that accompany such an understanding. There are consequences to the very

1. Lewis, *Screwtape Letters*, 188.
2. Bonhoeffer, *Life Together*, 30.

way we order such matters. It makes a difference whether or not we fundamentally see the church *as* a service to our neighboring communities, issues of "faith" being more private and personal in nature. It effects the whole orientation of our being if we see the church *as* an act called "declaration."

It is rather within the embrace of *beholding God* that the other emphases are understood, critical as they are. Spiritual formation and growth is that particular shape which is commensurate with being transformed *according to the Son*. Extending a tender hand of love and comfort is true to the one who abides *in the Spirit*, the comforter and counselor. Mission and proclamation are specific responses to the present world in order to draw all nations to *hallow the Father*. So long as these infinitely important tasks are not related back to their end in *beholding God*, they will forever misconstrue the nature of reality itself and thereby continue to reap from an unsightly harvest. Distinctly Christian unity cannot be established on secondary grounds. As a people, our purpose, identity, and meaning do not rest on that which is realized by our efforts; rather we are to be participants in a definite reality made possible by God.

The Woman Who Gave More

However, before one laments the ethereal way in which the church has hitherto be articulated, we shall consider those instances of divine clarity that Christ brought to our attention. We attend the women who gave more.

As Jesus lifted his eyes to observe the rich placing gifts into an offering box, he beheld in addition "a poor widow" who contributed merely two copper coins into the treasury (Luke 21:2). Compelled by the occasion, he spoke an intriguing and properly captivating word to those present. "Truly" Jesus said, this "poor widow has put in more than all of them" (Luke 21:3). For indeed Jesus argued, those offering from the bounty of their lavish estates submit only a fraction, a minor piece, of their "abundance." On the contrary, the woman—the "poor widow"—contributed "out of her poverty" and "has put in all she had to live on" (Luke 21:4).

A True Offering

On one level, this entirely tender woman has satisfied for us the requirement unto obedience, that scandalizing command on our lives to *follow*. She has given to God what is God's, reserved and withheld nothing for herself, and been wise and attentive with her possessions even during times of impoverishment, maintaining focus upon the Lord. But this woman invites us to consider her life in infinitely greater detail.

And while she is exemplary in these ways, we have reason to pause over the grandeur of the religious demand; surely this woman is not praiseworthy as one who reiterates oppressive expectations resembling those of the Pharisees: who "tie up heavy burdens, hard to bear, and lay them on people's shoulders" though "they themselves are not willing to move them with their finger" (Matt 23:4 ESV). Rather, Jesus peers ever truly into her being and delights in the gentleness of her soul. For her "heavy burden" exudes divine freedom, and it is just such a freedom that makes peaceful subordination possible. As Jesus declares, we are not to "resist" an evil one, turning and providing the other cheek to the one who strikes us, offering our coat to the one desiring to take it, dwelling for two miles with the one who demands we go one, and giving to the one who seeks to beg and borrow (Matt 5:39–42); all things considered, Jesus teaches us to respond to a world of violence by "providing," "offering," "dwelling," and "giving." It is such a freedom whereby even slaves can endure with patience the authority of masters "with all deference, not only those who are kind and gentle but also those who are harsh" (1 Pet 2:18). This freedom subjects us to the "governing authorities" (Rom 13:1), compels us to love our enemies and "pray for those who persecute" us (Matt 5:44), and liberates us to "render to Caesar the things that are Caesars" (Luke 20:25). Therefore, the poor widow offers a free and gratuitous gift out of the exceeding spiritual wealth she possesses: "Then Jesus said to the Jews who had believed in him, 'If you continue in my word, you are truly my disciples; and you will know the truth, and the truth will make you free . . . [and] if the Son makes you free, you will be free indeed'" (John 8:31–32, 36).

Moreover, that description—"she out of her poverty has put in all she had"—resounds with christological fortuity; for she reiterates that perichoretic exchange in the life of God, the fullness resultant from kenotic adoration, and thereby repeats the triune life of the divine Son. For in as much as we contemplate the divine nature, we should regard that nature as intelligible according to the liveliness of its very essence. In other words, the divine nature is not sufficiently coherent independent from triune existence. It is not simply a substance in which the divine persons can be said to share. Rather, it is in the traversing of that infinite distance and difference that love abides, the peaceful and delightful radiance of seeing the otherness of the other. And within this threefold traversal, the divine nature is exposited: "As the God who gives a difference that is more than merely negative and that opens out analogically from the 'theme' he imparts (the theme of free differentiation, orientated in love toward the other and all), he shows that difference is—still more radically, more originally—peace and joy."[3] In this way, the poor widow is demonstrative of that pure and sensible fullness that is the outpouring of attention toward the beautiful: an instance of worship.

As a repetition of the divine Son—seen by and reflective of the Father, known and adorned by the Spirit—the woman weds heaven and earth. Though she has little of which to boast, she assembles what is in her possession and orders them into their proper place. By drawing up her earthy abode into the prostration of reverence, she unifies her place with its truest form understood within the divine embrace. It is precisely in beholding God that she has reconciled the world. The mundane, ordinary, and unsightly moments of finitude are made occasions of peace which radiate with splendor the divine nature exposited by the self-outpouring of the Son. The poor widow redeemed the world.

3. Hart, *Beauty of the Infinite*, 181.

Worthy of Heaven

Indeed, this offering is didactic regarding the works and ways of the divine economy. For, it is the fount of adoration which springs forth a noble gift, the trivial amount (two copper coins) being transposed by the life given it. Jesus tells us that the woman "put in more than all of them" (Luke 21:3), and while its significance is initially predicated upon its relative worth to the women, the offering itself is representative of true worship ripened by a humble and contrite spirit. On the contrary, the offering of the rich does not achieve the acknowledgment of the Lord in so far as it communicates the internal affairs of those so giving: "The good person out of the good treasure of the heart produces good, and the evil person out of evil treasure produces evil; for it is out of the abundance of the heart that the mouth speak" (Luke 6:45); "Are grapes gathered from thorns, or figs from thistles? In the same way, every good tree bears good fruit, but the bad tree bears bad fruit" (Matt 7:16–17). And, as Cain heard in response to his failed offering: "If you do well, will you not be accepted?" (Gen 4:7). What is to be noticed here is that what a thing "is" remains a matter of infinite perspective, the veil of materiality only serves to hinder what can be said to be *true*; for she has made of the world that which it is. Therefore, what "is" the church? The church is that body whose shape and dwelling is the infinite traversal of splendor and grace, knowing and known by God, and contradicting of its appearances, plain and uninspired as they may be.

The occasion also teaches us something of the fruit of impoverishment. However, in making such a claim we are to be obsessively conscientious of what this does and does not mean, for how perverse and ignorant it would be to praise the slums from atop the city palace. Rather, what this statement suggests is that the poor are not seduced under the allure of self-sufficiency, they are not distracted from understanding their lives as being *unto* another. And while impoverishment is symptomatic of a world withstanding its cosmic birth pains (Rom 8:22), the poor are well prepared to "be" unto God—a choice analogy by the Lord himself.

For we are sobered by the voice of the "rich man" calling to Abraham requesting that he send forth Lazarus: "I beg you to send him to my father's house—for I have five brothers—that he may warn them, so that they will not also come into this place" (Luke 16:27–28). But Abraham said unto him that even if one should rise from the dead and plead with them face-to-face, they would still be blinded by the shimmer of their "fine" and "purple" linen, groggy from their daily feasts and festivals, and unaware that their very being "is" a fullness in self-giving—a rhapsodic appraisal in deferential awe. This is depicted with precision as the passage tells of Lazarus "who longed to satisfy his hunger," a phrase so tantalizingly open to plain and spiritual implications, with "what fell from the rich man's table," evincing that excessive and unaware nature (Luke 16:21).

So it is with the poor widow. Her perceptive spirit enables her to give all the more. For, as the rich amass their wealth they are tempted to think that this provides opportunity to give in abundance; however, it is the woman who knows that her existence is a transcendent and open posture, and therefore she evaluates the worth of her offering according to the incomparable wealth of God's limitless bounty—an evaluation that only the "poor" can make. The rich have bent their spiritual vision toward the emptiness of material goods, and thereby in giving a portion of their wealth they surrender an invaluable fragment of their life's meaning: they "give" more than can be imagined. So in the end, the woman has put in the least of all, as comprehended alongside the divine magnitude; however, God reveals this least to be *truly* great.

It is these through whom the divine light brightens the world. For light is not merely the desirable end of a moral continuum but the bringing to bear what is, the unveiling and revealing of the way things are. It is to uncover the reflective and hospitable shape of creation, a spacious abode for the divine weight: "You are the light of the world. A city built on a hill cannot be hid" (Matt 5:14). As the Apostle Paul suggests: "Even though our outer nature is wasting away, our inner nature is being renewed day by day. For this slight momentary affliction is preparing us for an eternal

Church

weight of glory beyond all measure, because we look not at what can be seen but at what cannot be seen; for what can be seen is temporary, but what cannot be seen is eternal" (2 Cor 4:16–18). It is our prerogative to be those seeking the "things that are above," setting our minds upon them (Col 3:2). For even though we do not now see Jesus Christ, we love him, believe in him, and rejoice with "an indescribable and glorious joy" (1 Pet 1:7–8). And thus we are "holy"—likened unto our heavenly Father, "You shall be holy, for I am holy" (1 Pet 1:15)—being those who are "sanctified in Christ Jesus" (1 Cor 1:1), living our lives in "reverent fear" (1 Pet 1:17). And having "purified" our souls we "love one another deeply from the heart . . . [being] born anew, not of perishable but of imperishable seed" (1 Pet 1:17). Therefore, walking in the light "as he himself is in the light, we have fellowship" (1 John 1:7), being built into a "spiritual house" made of living stones offering living sacrifices (1 Pet 2:4–5): "You are a chosen race, a royal priesthood, a holy nation, God's own people, in order that you may proclaim the mighty acts of him who called you out of darkness into his marvelous light" (1 Pet 2:9). Therefore we are those who hallow the Father in the Spirit according to the Son and thereby behold God; the church "is" the poor widow who gave all she had to live on.

In Memory of Her

We are reminded of that other saintly gesture that cannot go untold. As Jesus was preparing for his impending death, Mary took a pound of "pure" and "costly" perfume (John 12:3) and proceeded to anoint him for burial, spreading over him a mixture of tears and ointment. Among the outbursts of petition from those present Jesus says, she "has done a beautiful thing to me" (Mark 14:6 ESV). Like the poor widow, the radiance of this blessed woman occasions only a thin veil between heaven and earth; and in a spiritually inviting phrase, John tells us that "the house was filled with the fragrance" (John 12:3). Therefore, Jesus declares that wherever the "gospel is proclaimed in the whole world" that which she has done will be told "in memory of her" (Matt 26:13). Blessed are the beautiful, for they shall never be forgotten: "His bride has made herself ready" (Rev 19:7).

There is thus only one way to wisdom: awe. Forfeit your sense of awe, let your conceit diminish your ability to revere, and the universe becomes a market place for you. The loss of awe is the great block to insight. A return to reverence is the first prerequisite for a revival of wisdom, for the discovery of the world as an allusion to God. Wisdom comes from awe rather than from shrewdness. It is evoked not in moments of calculation but in moments of being in rapport with the mystery of reality. The greatest insights happen to us in moments of awe. A moment of awe is a moment of self-consecration. They who sense the wonder share in the wonder. They who keep holy the things that are holy shall themselves become holy.

—ABRAHAM HESCHEL[4]

---

4. *God in Search of Man*, 78.

9
Eschatology

Ascribe to the Lord, O heavenly beings, ascribe to the Lord glory and strength. Ascribe to the Lord the glory of his name; worship the Lord in holy splendor.... The Lord sits enthroned over the flood; the Lord sits enthroned as king forever. May the Lord give strength to his people! May the Lord bless his people with peace!

—PSALM 29:1–2, 10–11

With all wisdom and insight he has made known to us the mystery of his will, according to his good pleasure that he set forth in Christ, as a plan for the fullness of time, to gather up all things in him, things in heaven and things on earth. In Christ we have also obtained an inheritance, having been destined according to the purpose of him who accomplishes all things according to his counsel and will.

—EPHESIANS 1:8–11

AMID THE TALES OF terror for which there is no ending, there beckons a voice, as of one crying in the wilderness: "Then I saw." For all that transpires without plot, for all that is endured without reason, there is a true tale which ends with grace and grandeur. For at the summation of those petitions which sought God in a godless place, inquired of hope when it seemed incomprehensible, and lamented in utter dereliction comes the appearing—the arriving—of what is new. "Then I saw a new heaven and a new earth; for the first heaven and the first earth had passed away, and the sea was no more. And I saw the holy city, the new Jerusalem, coming down out of heaven from God, prepared as a bride adorned for her husband" (Rev 21:1-2).

Without continuity or strife, God bestows upon his people. Recalling the divine impetus of the original act of creation itself— a voluntary, free, and benevolent act—thus we regard the "new" creation (the final, fulfilled, and eschatological work of God). In form and content the nature of the work is reminiscent and expressive of the God we have come to know in Christ. For the end is like the beginning, an act out of will of the creator God, the one who is above and before all things. The heavenly city exudes gift, a gift moreover that is touched by the tenderness of God who *adorns* the city. And as gift, it refuses to be the result, product, or achievement of human ends. It does not arise on account of our efforts. It is properly gratuitous. In this way therefore it is not the manifestation our living out the kingdom, nor is it the consummation of a process of strife. It is an eschaton fitting for a people who relinquish control for gentleness.

The brilliance of the city, descending in glory from on high, is in addition discriminatory. As is the nature of God's light, there is a judgment consequent to the truth. For those tales of hopelessness which are contradicted by hope are not alone, the array of false and fancy tales come up against the one, true, elect account. The breaking of the dawn is the shrinking of the night, and "there will be no night" (Rev 21:25). To the one who deals not with truth, beauty, and goodness, the beatific is condemning: as it is written, "the appearance of the glory of the Lord was like a devouring fire on the top of the mountain in the sight of the people of Israel" (Exod 24:17). This ought to guide our understanding of judgment: for "Love is the source and the basis of the possibility of the wrath of God. The opposite of love is not wrath, but indifference."[1] Some exhibit a morose clinging to those deceiving stories and ends

---

1. Moltmann, *Crucified God*, 272.

Eschatology

which bemoan the light of God's kingdom. Such are those who have fingers sinking ever deeply into the fleshy décor of earth's outerwear, knowing the freedom of God only as an affront to all they are: God's offer is a threat, his truth is compromising, and his desires are dubious: "With the merciful you show yourself merciful; with the blameless man you show yourself blameless; with the purified you show yourself pure; and with the crooked you make yourself seem tortuous" (Ps 18:25–26 ESV).

For the "polluted" will be the end of pollution, "end" being both its extinguishment and *telos* (its undifferentiated demise and fulfillment) as evil *is* the privation of Being. For like a thief in the night the owner of the home returns only to find strangers occupying his place, glorying in their shame and celebrating abominable deeds. What good is the graciousness of the king to those who seek only his throne? God's heavenly city is the narrative of election, inhabited by Christ, the Elect One, and the bride, his elect people: "And I heard a loud voice from the throne saying, 'Behold, the dwelling place of God is with [humanity]. He will dwell with them, and they will be his people, and God himself will be with them as their God. He will wipe away every tear from their eyes, and death shall be no more, neither shall there be mourning, nor crying, nor pain anymore, for the former things have passed away'" (Rev 21:3–4 ESV).

And It Was Very Good

It is altogether enthralling to image what such bliss might be like, recounting the instances of spiritual intimacy or the glorious impact of nature's greatest sights. Moreover, that new dwelling is described as having "no temple in the city, for its temple is the Lord God the Almighty and the Lamb. And the city has no need of sun or moon to shine on it, for the glory of God is its light, and its lamp is the Lamb. The nations will walk by its light, and the kings of the earth will bring their glory into it" (Rev 21:22–24).

In our attempt to envision and describe just what kind of place this is, we are to keep one thing ever before us: that is to avoid the mistake of turning toward the creature rather than the creator, the thing created for the one who created. This is certainly our temptation at present. How easy it is to experience the joys earthy existence and be seduced into thinking such things hold the keys of life and happiness. In so far as we fail to regard Goodness, Truth, and Beauty as distinguished and proper ends, which grace our being in the advent of their appearing, we fail to separate the idol from the image, the pot from the potter. As genuinely beautiful as a scene of rolling meadows may be, we are to resist considering their beauty as a contained possession which emanates from the scene itself. Rather it is the Christian witness that testifies to the One who is Beauty—simple and pure—in whom creation is embraced. The Good is formally set apart as the limitless shape and end of all, it embraces but does not reside within the created thing. Therefore, whatever might be said of the *new* creation, the splendid and heavenly city, it must be contested that the city radiates with this formal rhetoric, the God-ness of all Goodness. In this way, there is no *light* other than the one who *is* the light of the world. There is no designated locus for worship (i.e., the temple) because God has realized creation's doxological being, a being that in every way knows, loves, and pursues the Holy One.

So is the essence of the infinite. Because it is truly transcendent it is immanent, near yet ever and always out of reach. And as such, it is an affront to all attempts to pillage and plunder. The infinite is not merely an essence that is full in itself but merely at a distance from us, rather it is by its essence complete distance and otherness. It is therefore reality imposing upon our deception the truth of Being: we do not sequentially and materially comprise reality nor are we supremely powerful so as to attain our own destiny, the infinite is a teacher of how we exist without ever obtaining, controlling, or manipulating the One. We learn that life is a gracious and boundless pursuit of the Good, the unending embrace which never overcomes distance. In this way we repeat the dynamism of the divine life, and in this way we may regard the *beauty of the infinite*.[2]

2. From the title of David Bentley Hart's *The Beauty of the Infinite*.

Eschatology

And yet hope, like all good things, is vulnerable to corruption. For while hope is an integral feature of our way in the world, it will not correct our idolizing tendencies of directing our soul to that which is other than God. It does not require a particularly virtuous individual to abide by heavenly fantasies conveniently catered to their own tastes. Thus "heaven" can be employed for any range of curious ends, from the inventive to the suspect.

Therefore, hope needs to be taught. It needs a conscientious balance distinguishing between that holy bliss to which our soul appropriately longs—the triune life in which we provisionally share—and the eschatological dwelling that will facilitate the radiance of God. We must not lose sight of the fact that God and God alone is our portion, our stay, our blessedness. And it would be to our detriment to allow a vision of the afterlife to distract us from our hearts true lover, to allow heaven to rob us of worship.

Therefore we rest in God, the one who is our delight, and yet that delight is what informs our sorrowful protest of earth's atrocities. Our desire for the one who is Good neither removes us from the world nor engenders apathy toward it, for it is love that seeks peace at all costs. And "peace" is not merely the spiritual accomplishment of being distracted from the world, for even the Beloved Son "descended" upon a hostile world. Rather peace rests upon promise, a promise that there shall one day be no more tears, a promise that our own "descending" into the world is not in vain, a promise that we shall behold our God face-to-face. In this way, hope is our very life.

Some Will Be Raised

For all that is blessed about that heavenly spectacle, there nevertheless remains a daunting absence of "some," those for whom life was no gift. Among those crimes and vices which plague humanity, at work in the world is an *evangel* of death.

And whether it begins with a subtle doubting of God's moral character, or a skepticism toward all things "supernatural," or perhaps a spiritualization of the bliss of "nothingness," this *evangel* propagates an ultimate discontinuity between this world and the next. And by doubting the credibility of any intelligible *after*life, it must invest its interests elsewhere and devise the world according to a definite and certain end that awaits. An end so conceived will hover over life's events uttering cruel remarks of temporality and finitude, ever reminding joy of its destination. It is then, after nothingness has ridiculed all behavior governed by purpose, that what is left of the human person appears to be no more than an instant in the barrage of being. The weight and measure of all things is calibrated according to the backdrop of life's inevitable end.

And with that end permanently fixed ahead, the hero is no longer the one who sacrifices in light of future glory, for they know only the tragedy of missing life's small offerings, rather the hero is the one who learns to live in the face of death-unapologetically owning death as that which is integral to life. Thus life is deemed precious *because* it is limited, and all strides in virtue seek to contribute to the quality of that life for subsequent generations. And while an investment to be sure, this desire continues to perpetuate the absolutizing of nothingness—the great judge of life's ventures. In this way, the supreme expression of charity is giving oneself entirely for another, attaining "purpose" in the selfless attention toward the other. However, what is lost in this charitable exchange is that which is to be *given*. If one's purpose is no more than bestowing what is best on others, they will in fact only transfer an understanding that there is nothing *beyond* that is worth pursuing for themselves. Therefore, tragically, charity becomes the omen of meaninglessness.

What then is left is to make of nothingness a romantic though solemn conclusion. It is the undifferentiating unity of all that saves from the violence of existence. It is the great equalizer that keeps honest the proud, and in its own way provides togetherness in the darkened synergy of all being. Therefore, in propagating discontinuity, this *evangel* has confused death for bliss and thereby works to convince the world that it is a living contradiction: *finding* purpose and *creating* meaning within the confines of finitude.

Eschatology

Therefore as the church extends the blessedness of hope it becomes divine rhetoric, compelling the world to consider life *after* death as a people who dare to be more. "Beloved, build yourselves up on your most holy faith; pray in the Holy Spirit; keep yourselves in the love of God; look forward to the mercy of our Lord Jesus Christ that leads to eternal life. And have mercy on some who [doubt]" (Jude 20-22). That "divine rhetoric," *in* and not *of* the world, is none other than the reiteration of the eternal Word, "I came that they may have life, and have it abundantly" (John 10:10).

The soul now feels that it is all inflamed in the divine union and that its palate is all bathed in glory and love, that in the most intimate part of its substance it is flooded with no less than rivers of glory, abounding in delights, and that from its bosom flow rivers of living water [John 7:38], which the Son of God declared will rise up in such souls. Accordingly it seems, because the soul is so vigorously transformed in God, so sublimely possessed by him and arrayed with such rich gifts and virtues, that it is singularly close to beatitude—so close that only a thin veil separates it.

—JOHN OF THE CROSS[3]

---

3. *Living Flame of Love*, 113.

10
Prolegomena

> Who are they that fear the Lord? He will teach them the way that they should choose. They will abide in prosperity, and their children shall possess the land. The friendship of the Lord is for those who fear him, and he makes his covenant known to them. My eyes are ever toward the Lord.
>
> —PSALM 25:12–15

> I pray that, according to the riches of his glory, he may grant that you may be strengthened in your inner being with power through his Spirit, and that Christ may dwell in your hearts through faith, as you are being rooted and grounded in love. I pray that you may have the power to comprehend, with all the saints, what is the breadth and length and height and depth, and to know the love of Christ that surpasses knowledge, so that you may be filled with all the fullness of God.
>
> —EPHESIANS 3:16–19

THE WORD "PROLEGOMENA" USUALLY designates that front matter which serves to introduce a theological tome. It attempts to give prior explanations that may not be handled thoroughly throughout the work itself but nevertheless require attention. In some ways, it is a justification—or rather delineation—of what is going to be said. More than offering further information on the topic, it explains how it is that we should be related to the truth in question at all. Therefore, it may appear rather odd to address these matters at the conclusion. However, we end off as we began: *It is in the place of aftermath that we are most ably equipped to speak to God's ineffable qualities. Should we have had no resources to draw from, nor encounter upon which to reflect, there would remain no certainty as to whether a thing called "God" is tangible.*

Psalm 139: God's Thoughts

The psalm is likely a familiar one, and for good reason; it has a range of intriguing material: from the existential angst of one crying out unto God to racy suggestions many of us would personally rather omit. We have the interesting feature that just before the psalmist asks God to "search" and "try" him, he speaks about hating "them" with a "complete hatred"—a comment that appears to be in no little need of refinement.

And yet we are drawn to the psalmist's concern that his thoughts be known and tried by nothing less than God's own thoughts. In fact, this desire is woven throughout the prayer. For even that which we call "darkness" is "not dark to you [that is the LORD]" for "the night is bright as the day" (Ps 139:12). Moreover, the "hidden" and "secret" place that is a mother's womb is exposed and essentially public for God. He not only sees, but is active and at work forming, knitting, weaving (Ps 139:13–15). Before "I" was formed, says the psalmist, the LORD had written "all the days that were formed for me" (Ps 139:16).

God reframes our world and our perception according to his perspective, which is distinct and not limited to our own. This emphasis extends to all regions, familiar and otherwise: should we go to the heavens, the LORD is there; should we go to the depths of Sheol, the LORD is there, also; what therefore remains "unreachable" that God himself has not reached? "Such knowledge is too wonderful for me; it is so high that I cannot attain it" (v. 6).

What is more, God's thoughts not only comprehend those things which are by nature out of our grasp—even if we should take the wings of the morning to dwell in the uttermost parts of the sea (Ps 139:9)—but they shape how we see "plain" reality. Notice how the brute fact of childbirth is conceived of quite specifically, namely that which is delicately fashioned, fearfully and wonderfully, by the creative works of God's tender hands (Ps 139:14). The natural world is not best understood as "nature" but apprehended as *creation*. In other words, God's thoughts give us the proper lens with which to see the world. In the book of Isaiah we read: "My thoughts are not your thoughts, nor are your ways my ways, says the Lord. For as the heavens are higher than the earth, so are my ways higher than your ways and my thoughts than your thoughts" (Isa 55:8–9). And as the Apostle Paul continues on the same theme, "no one comprehends what is truly God's except the Spirit of God. Now we have received not the spirit of the world, but the Spirit that is from God, so that we may understand the gifts bestowed on us by God. And we speak of these things in words not taught by human wisdom but taught by the Spirit, interpreting spiritual things to those who are spiritual" (1 Cor 2:11–13).

It is therefore no coincidence that the opening and concluding lines of this Psalm frame the material in the context of one contrite, reverent, and essentially prayerful before the LORD: the opening words, "O LORD, you have searched me and know me," correspond with the final verses, "Search me, O God, and know my heart; test me and know my thoughts. See if there is any wicked way in me, and lead me in the way everlasting" (Ps 139:23–24). It is here, recognizing the convergence of God's thoughts and our praying, that we begin our reflection on knowledge.

The Unforgivable Sin

After ascending upon the mountain and calling unto himself "twelve," Jesus went home, at which time the crowd gathered again making a boisterous assembly to the point that those present were unable even to eat (Mark 3:20). And as Jesus was exchanging

Prolegomena

among those within the crowd, his family came out to "seize him" having heard the noise. Curiously, his family was concerned saying, "He has gone out of his mind" (Mark 3:21).

Meanwhile the scribes from Jerusalem were challenging Jesus on behalf of the miraculous and wondrous things he had been doing, suggesting that he was possessed by "Beelzebul" and that "by the ruler of the demons he casts out demons" (Mark 3:22). Jesus retorted in parable: "How can Satan cast out Satan? If a kingdom is divided against itself, that kingdom cannot stand. And if a house is divided against itself, that house will not be able to stand. And if Satan has risen up against himself and is divided, he cannot stand, but his end has come. But no one can enter a strong man's house and plunder his property without first tying up the strong man; then indeed the house can be plundered" (Mark 3:23–27).

Jesus is at once balancing a condemning counterargument and a prophetic injunction. For, he presumes the strength of "Satan's" kingdom as he mutes their suggestion that Jesus' exorcisms were accomplished by the power of Satan—how then would such a "strong" kingdom remain if its own rebel against it? Moreover, he insightfully plays off the occasion. For if Satan's kingdom *was* divided, that would mean "he cannot stand" and his "end has come" (Mark 3:26), which would also imply that someone has "plundered" the "strong man's house" (Mark 3:27). And it is that biting remark that brings to mind the actual and effective power at work through Jesus himself, Beelzebul's or not. Satan's kingdom *is* coming to an end, but not on account of division.

Just then, Jesus makes a remarkable and terrifying claim: "'Truly I tell you, people will be forgiven for their sins and whatever blasphemies they utter; but whoever blasphemes against the Holy Spirit can never have forgiveness, but is guilty of an eternal sin'—for they had said, 'He has an unclean spirit'" (Mark 3:28–30). What was it precisely that incited an absolutizing condemnation such as this?

When Jesus speaks, there is an implicit and explicit invitation to those who have "ears to hear" (Mark 4:9), for he is well aware of those in his midst who indeed "look, but not perceive," "listen, but not understand" (Mark 4:12). And it is this irony that he uses elsewhere; for in healing a blind beggar Jesus praises the man's capacity to "perceive" him in his glory (John 9:37), adding that his own coming has been in order that "those who do not see may see" (John 9:39). Hearing this, the Pharisees presumptuously revolt by saying, "Surely we are not blind, are we?" (John 9:40). Jesus then uses the example of the blind man to say that if only they were indeed "blind" they would see and therefore "not have sin," but precisely *because* they think they see their "sin remains" (John 9:41). For having come to make the blind see, he also has come that "those who do see may become blind" (John 9:39).

Because the Pharisees cannot *see* in the works of Jesus anything other than fraudulent, deceptive, and suspect origins, they cannot and will not *perceive* the divine light which emanates from Jesus' life. And in so failing to understand, they stare directly in the face of God and call his ways and works demonic. Their "sin remains"—or rather, they are guilty of an "eternal sin" because— they refuse to see forgiveness. For "the light shineth in darkness; and the darkness comprehended it not" (John 1:5 KJV). Therefore, it is God's singular presence which bequeaths judgment on the wicked and life on the righteous: "Those who believe in him are not condemned; but those who do not believe are condemned already" (John 3:18); for "this is the judgment, that the light has come into the world, and people loved darkness rather than light" (John 3:19). This unforgivable sin does not find much precedence throughout Scripture, but in Isaiah we read, "they rebelled and grieved his holy spirit; therefore he became their enemy" (Isa 63:10). And in light of what has been revealed in Christ Jesus, it no longer remains clear whether God turned in becoming their enemy or whether they so become in their own rebelling.

Having contested his identity, his mother and his brother finally make it through and request a meeting with him; Jesus responds, "'Who are my mother and my brothers?' And looking at those who sat around him, he said, 'Here are my mother and my brothers!'" (Mark 3:33–34).

Prolegomena

The Beginning of Knowledge

We may be among those quick to ridicule the "blind" Pharisees for failing to grasp the obvious reality standing plainly before their eyes. But what then do we make of all the beauty in the world that is trampled underfoot by the ungrateful and self-seeking ignorance that is our everyday, or the moments when we profane the gratuity of God's love for others by our short tempers and lengthy demands, or perhaps the mockery that is resultant from our failing to bear responsibility—appealing often to one excuse after another? We fail to "know" reality because reality is magnificently arrayed, requiring souls that are as equally splendid.

The great tradition has regarded Truth, Goodness, Beauty, One, and Being as proper transcendentals. And while distinguishable, they are truly inseparable. There is a unique flavor to each aspect, but they are inconceivable in pure isolation because in fact they are neither isolated nor composite. Knowing the "truth" is to know it as it exists by its other aspects, its aesthetic and perfect features. And it is not as though truth is contextualized by the others, as if truth ought to be spoken "in love"; rather, *there is no truth apart from love*. Therefore, when it is contested by Scripture and the tradition that holiness is the precondition for knowledge it does not intend to suggest that is it morally responsible or a noble attitude, it means that holiness is required precisely because Being is sacred: "The fear of the Lord is the beginning of knowledge; fools despise wisdom and instruction" (Prov 1:7). As the writer of Hebrews contests, "Let us give thanks, by which we offer to God an acceptable worship with reverence and awe" (Heb 12:28).

Because reality is adorned, the capacity to *convey* that reality is predicated upon our manner. For "who is wise and understanding among you? Show by your good life that your works are done with gentleness born of wisdom" (Jas 3:13). And while there is that type of "knowledge" which puffs up, it is neither "come down from above" (Jas 3:15) nor "pure, then peaceable, gentle, willing to yield, full of mercy and good fruits, without a trace of partiality or hypocrisy" (Jas 3:17). In other words, it is no knowledge at all, merely foolishness. True knowledge is that which bears meekness; it bears meekness precisely because meekness coveys the manner of reality: it conveys who and what God is.

As Peter admonishes those under various social pressures, he calls for "a tender heart, and a humble mind" (1 Pet 3:8); and with regard to the Christian testimony he says, "In your hearts sanctify Christ as Lord. Always be ready to make your defense to anyone who demands from you an accounting for the hope that is in you" (1 Pet 3:15). How many with vigorous apologetic impulses have betrayed reality by attempting to conquer it? Their manner has fallen wholly out of sync with existence as they remain "false to the truth" (Jas 3:14). Rather, Peter adds to this admonition the single greatest qualifier of human conduct: "Yet do it with gentleness and reverence" (1 Pet 3:16).

Enfolded within the serenity of reverence is the entirety of Truth, Beauty, and Goodness. It is a transient confession of Being and beings. It speaks tenderly because it is all too vulnerably aware of one's own capacity for shortsightedness and folly, it regards life with the proportionate and enlightened consciousness of our contingency and our sanctity, and it renders a quiet brightness as it relays the giftedness of life and love. With wide-eyed wonder it tells the story of redemption, of gratuity, of desire; and it touches life with the widest gaze. Reverence capitulates the whole of reality according to its nature and thereby becomes the most indelible appearance of divine glory. By being neither narcissistic on account of affluence nor negated by poverty, reverence makes joy a corollary of unity with God and is ontologically legitimated by his immutable essence: it is the knowledge which saves from nihilism. "The friendship of the LORD is for those who fear him, and he makes his covenant known to them. *My eyes are ever toward the LORD*" (Ps 25:12–15). Reverence is a gaze which regards being in its proper light, seeing the world under, in, and with God. It is that decisive attention toward, ever beholding, the splendid at all times. The psalmist declares, "I have set the LORD always before me" (Ps 16:8); and this setting is that which conditions the right seeing.

Prolegomena

However, this beholding is nothing less than a discipline for which we owe our lives; and prayer is the practice of beholding God, and by learning to exist in prayer we learn how to live in the world. It is the place we sanctify for purity and keeping holy the things that are holy; it is where we are schooled by revering. Think of the innumerable consequences that result from never exercising life inextricably "in" God's presence—an unapologetic entrance of the *sanctum sanctorum*. How shall we ever behave toward God's gift of creation if we fail to ever behave toward God in himself? And as Bonhoeffer elucidates the meditative nature of prayer, reflecting on the lengthy prose of Psalm 119, he says: "Is this not an indication that prayer is not a matter of pouring out the human heart once and for all in need or joy, but of an unbroken, constant learning, accepting, and impressing upon the mind of God's will in Jesus Christ?"[1] Moreover, von Balthasar likewise affirms the centrality of prayer, "Thus the person who prays and who wants to gain a deeper understanding of the word [Logos] he desires to worship . . . will select with great care basic works for his studies which will observe the so-called exactitude of scholarship without losing sight of the most important exactitude, namely, the ordering of all thought toward prayer."[2] Therefore, reverence is the fruit of beholding in prayer, the majestic origin of knowledge.

Christ:
"Do not think, therefore, that you have found true peace if you feel no depression, or that all is well because you suffer no opposition. . . . For the true lover of virtue is not known by these things, nor do the progress and perfection of a man consist in them."

The Disciple:
"In what do they consist, Lord?"

1. Bonhoeffer, *Life Together*, 49.
2. Balthasar, *Prayer*, 226–27.

Behold Our God

> Christ:
> "They consist in offering yourself with all your heart to the divine will, not seeking what is yours either in small matters or great ones, either in temporal or eternal things, so that you will preserve equanimity and give thanks in both prosperity and adversity, seeing all things in their proper light."
>
> —THOMAS À KEMPIS[3]

---

3. *Imitation of Christ,* 73.

Epilogue

Throughout this work we have appealed to the past, to Scripture, to the experience of others. We have so related ourselves not merely because these references give us poignant metaphors or comprise our history, but because of the conviction that they, with us, share in the one reality that is the eternal and infinite God. And while there is uncertainty about the past and the experience of others, there is remarkable congruity which the Christian tradition suggests is borne of the transcending nature of humanity.

As we discern and appropriate the mystery of God revealed in and through Christ, we are enabled to perceive the divinity of being and the sacredness of existence. And in this way the contemplative and spiritual tradition gives the true impetus for love and justice. It remains unintelligible that one should divorce the ineffable, the meaningful, and the practical. Therefore in beholding our God we foster compassion for a world that is not yet itself.

APPENDIX A

On the Cruciformity of Knowledge

A Sermon

MARK 8:27-38

The Opaque God

A SUBTLE, YET LEADING, question, "Who do you say that I am?" A question filled with ramifications. This question was no doubt implied as Jesus approached the water's edge and addressed two men. Simon and Andrew are required to decide just who this man is, and upon charge to follow they respond, in the works of Mark, "immediately" (Mark 1:17-18).

While we may be tempted to congratulate these responsive disciples, we are stilled by the peculiar declaration of unclean spirits. For out of the mouth of a demon we hear, "I know who you are, the Holy One of God" (Mark 1:24). We need not travel very far to find differing accounts of just who Jesus really was. Perhaps Jesus was a great example in love and kindness: a picture of Jesus that is vague enough to gain wide acceptance, and avoid the awkward demand of faithfulness with our entire lives. Perhaps Jesus is the

APPENDIX A—*On the Cruciformity of Knowledge*

fiction of delusional cult leaders: a picture of Jesus that gives the whole Christian faith a smell of suspicion that blinds the world from his life and words—even when they are penetrating and profound.

It may be understandable that Jesus would have no patients for a demonic confession, but I suspect that his rebuke of Peter, the apostle, is beyond surprising. After all, trying to stop Jesus from death on a cross comes from the best of intensions. Who then would find fault in Peter who acts out of love and concern, who clearly desires what's best for Jesus? Before we too quickly point to the world for its false paintings of Jesus, let us recall that the great failing comes from Peter—the one who has committed himself to Jesus, who has chosen to follow him, and remains in his company.

It is Jesus' own sheep who are both in need of instruction, and are in danger of obstructing the very will of God. Jesus has been fitted to suit an endless variety of needs and desires. He has been made and remade into our image. While much, if not most, of Jesus is affirmed, there nevertheless remains material about his life we would rather neglect. We therefore are confronted, challenged by this story to acknowledge our blindness and learn to follow without presumption.

The occasion for Jesus' rebuke is Peter implying that he may determine how Jesus ought to behave, and consequently who Jesus ought to be—a fault that is no less tempting for us today. Yet what, above all, makes reading this passage difficult is for us to believe that we, along with Peter, should ever be called devils. Because, unless we appreciate that Jesus' severity is matched only by the severity of what is at stake, we will be at a loss in making sense of his harsh words. What is at stake is nothing less than the rejection of God himself.

Psalm 22 begins with a desolate and desperate cry unto the Lord. The cry is not unfamiliar to the brokenhearted, for with a voice resonating throughout the world, the psalmist cries out, "My God, my God, why have you forsaken me?" The tragic irony climaxes on the cross, as we find these words on the mouth of Jesus who has been forsaken by the world.

APPENDIX A—On the Cruciformity of Knowledge

Few temptations are as prominent as that of making God according to our desires: as Jesus suggests, having the mind on things of man, and not of God. It was this temptation that would face Samuel as he received the word of the Lord: in choosing a candidate who would be king over Israel the Lord declares, "Do not look on his appearance or on the height of his stature, because I have rejected him; for the LORD does not see as mortals sees; they look on the outward appearance, but the LORD looks on the heart" (1 Sam 16:7).

It was this temptation that would face a wondering Israel who would just as soon craft the image of a calf in the insecurity of Moses' absence (Exod 32). It was this temptation that would face the religious leaders of Jesus day. By adding to God's commands, the Pharisees turned God's good words of wisdom into cells of imprisonment. In one of his many conflicts with the Pharisees, Jesus says earlier in our Gospel, "You have a fine way of rejecting the commandment of God in order to keep your tradition!" (Mark 7:9). And quoting Isaiah, he also says, "This people honors me with their lips, but their hearts are far from me" (Mark 7:6).

Perhaps no greater confrontation between the mind of God and the mind of men is found then in Jesus' arrest. As he stood silent, like a lamb before the sheers, Pilot, face-to-face, "said to him, 'Do you refuse to speak to me? Do you not know that I have power to release you, and power to crucify you?' Jesus answered him, 'You would have no power over me unless it had been given you from above'" (John 19:10–11). *What is at stake is nothing less than the rejection of God himself.*

When Moses asked by what name he should know him by, the Lord replied, "I will be who I will be" (Exod 3:14). Israel had been invited as sojourners to learn who God was, yet it is the disciples who now struggle on that pilgrimage. Jesus' question, his subtle yet leading question, "Who do you say that I am?" (Mark 8:29), continues God's persistent challenge of our patients as we struggle keep up. In other words, we would have never looked for God on a cross except for the peculiar reality that that's precisely where he was.

APPENDIX A—*On the Cruciformity of Knowledge*

And because God so appeared among us, we are forever challenged to rethink our world. The way we consider greatness, achievement, and worth have all been put to death as foolish in light of Jesus suffering with the lowly. In this way, we are forever reminded that we need to be taught, and never may we assume.

To Behold His Glory

What then does it mean to know him? All pretense for flattery is confronted by the saying "If any want to become my followers, let them deny themselves and take up their cross and follow me" (Mark 8:34). When the Jewish leader Nicodemus pays Jesus the compliment of being the teacher from God, he oddly demands that Nicodemus be born again. Jesus demands that the life he now knows be put to death (John 3). "If anyone would come after me, let him deny himself and take up his cross and follow me" (Matt 16:24). Dietrich Bonhoeffer writes, "The cross is not the terrible end to an otherwise god-fearing and happy-life, but it meets us at the beginning of our communion with Christ. When Christ calls a man, he bids him come and die."[1]

But to what end? Why would God desire for us to suffer, to die, to be crucified? This death takes the form of a refusal. It is a refusal to exchange violence for violence. It is a refusal to secure food, shelter, and safety at the cost of violence. It is a refusal to prioritize careers over character. It is a refusal to demand what is due us. It is even the refusal to relish winning arguments—rejoicing in another's fault. It is the wholesale refusal to exchange peace for anything less. In this way, it is a choice of death for the flesh.

As Jesus says, "Verily, truly, I tell you, unless a grain of wheat falls into the earth and dies, it remains just a single grain; but if it dies, it bears much fruit" (John 12:24). We are "always carrying in the body the death of Jesus, so that the life of Jesus may also be made visible in our bodies" (2 Cor 4:10). When we examine ourselves in those moments when love is most difficult, we often find

1. Bonhoeffer, *Cost of Discipleship*, 79.

APPENDIX A—*On the Cruciformity of Knowledge*

an unwillingness to loosen our grip from something we deeply treasure. In our pride, we stubbornly demand upon our way, our reputation. In our fear, we shy from doing what is right to stay in that place we feel secure. In our anxiety, we lose sight of God's gentleness and assume control. In each case, we cling to what we feel will help us in the chaos of our lives, only to realize that by clinging to them, we deny Christ.

We choose hostility over love, destruction over life, and human stability over fellowship with a crucified Lord. "For those who want to save their life will lose it, and those who lose their life for my sake, and for the sake of the gospel, will save it. For what will it profit them to gain the whole world and forfeit their life?" (Mark 8:35–36). Such a demand is altogether troubling, and even strange, if we fail to see here the goodness of God.

God's radical calling could very quickly become a reason to believe he is first demanding and harsh and then perhaps loving of those who do as he says. As the holy God who demands a certain righteousness, too many fathers, mothers, pastors, priests, teachers, leaders, and counselors have made God to be harsh and arbitrary. However, a command will continue to be abused so long as it stands divorced from the love of its giver. Jesus' demand that we submit ourselves to death continually for his sake is not arbitrary or cruel; it is precisely for the purpose of life: life eternal, life in love, life to the fullest. For in union with Christ, we know inextricable joy by his friendship, eternal hope by his resurrection, and peacemaking love by his Spirit.

For, what is it that could make possible a people who decide to give—even at their own expense? People who determine to move their homes into impoverished areas in order to fellowship with the broken? Who learn to increasingly regard as gift, not only possessions but their own company—and seek to bestow that on others? What could make possible a people who seek with intentionality to identify the burdens of the world—and help bear up under them? It is the recognition that we have given up our lives.

In each circumstance, we regard our lives as that which has been surrendered. And in so doing, we claim the joy, honesty, and

APPENDIX A—*On the Cruciformity of Knowledge*

clarity of simply following Jesus. The ongoing struggle we have in determining to what extent I am willing to follow him is meant to be left behind, as our old lives have so been. As Paul contests, "I appeal to you therefore, brothers and sisters, by the mercies of God, to present your bodies as a living sacrifice, holy and acceptable to God, which is your spiritual worship. Do not be conformed to this world, but be transformed by the renewing of your minds, so that you may discern what is the will of God—what is good and acceptable and perfect" (Rom 12:1–2). And in his wonderful and encouraging letter to the Philippians, he recounts the way in which his life is conducted as having already been given in Christ. Paul, writing from prison says, "Whatever gains I had, these I have come to regard as loss because of Christ. More than that, I regard everything as loss because of the surpassing value of knowing Christ Jesus my Lord. For his sake I have suffered the loss of all things, and I regard them as rubbish, in order that I may gain Christ" (Phil 3:7–8).

And yet, we are compelled to confession. We cannot rely on our own judgment as to what such a life should look like. And we ought to fear all the ways we will take occasion to lessen, and cheapen, the life of discipleship. Our capacity for self-deception is all too real. It is for this reason that the church is essential. As we uphold one another through the declaration of God's word, we learn to speak honestly—to speak truly—to one another. Through the ongoing formation of the community, we realize with increasing clarity what is entailed in discipleship. With humility we admit that we require others to tell us what this looks like for our own life. In addition, we each bear the burden of speaking truthfully to one another. Lest we, with Peter, be called God's enemy.

Therefore in response to Jesus' question "Who do you say that I am?," we answer, "He will be who he will be."

APPENDIX A—*On the Cruciformity of Knowledge*

Work your good will,
Give us eyes to notice what can be seen of you,
Give us faith to trust what stays hidden of you,
Give us nerve to obey you this day,
Even where we do not see."

—WALTER BRUEGGEMANN[2]

---

2. *Awed to Heaven*, 45.

APPENDIX B

Gregory of Nyssa

A Sermon on the Sixth Beatitude

> Blessed are the pure in heart,
> for they shall see God.
>
> —MATTHEW 5:8[1]

OVERCOME BY THE GRANDEUR of such a statement, Gregory of Nyssa relates his encounter to one peering over a high mountain range down upon the vastness of the ocean, for the beatitude conjures those images and instances that exhibit finite immensity—those corporeal lessons in wonder: "That is what my mind feels when it peers down from the loftiness of the Lord's saying, as from a mountain peak, upon the infinite depth of thought to which it gives vantage."[2] There is indeed nothing short of "awesome implications," says Gregory to the conjecture "they shall see God," as "God offers himself as a spectacle for those whose hearts are purified."[3] And while Gregory exercises a certain luxury as he delineates the experience of knowing and seeing God—that is, as

1. Scripture quotations are taken directly from the Gregory of Nyssa text.
2. Gregory of Nyssa, *Sermon on the Sixth Beatitude*, 29.
3. Ibid.

APPENDIX B—*Gregory of Nyssa*

a theologian of that glorious patristic period—his voice is not met by our contemporaries with the same familiarity it might have once had. While "God" is certainly not absent from the lives of Christians, we might confess that a properly beatific *telos* is rather foreign to our existence.

However, one may object—as Gregory himself notes—by pointing to those "pillars of the faith" who "unanimously pronounce [seeing God] unattainable."[4] The great Apostle John suggests: "No one has ever seen God" (John 1:18); the sublime Apostle Paul adds, God "whom no one has seen or can see" (1 Tim 6:16); and finally, Moses declares that "no one can see God and live" (Exod 33:20). God is hence likened unto that smooth rock who withstands attempts to be grasped and secured.[5] We, after all, are likely more comfortable with the unpresuming posture that accompanies such "humble" claims, however it is a false humility that concedes to the skeptical affirmation of undifferentiated sublimity.

For these negative assessments do not make up the entirety of the Christian witness. Gregory identifies the inherent tension between the impossibility and necessity of seeing God, as seeing God *is* eternal life.[6] Much like Peter, the Lord sustains our "faltering hope"; for the pure of heart are "blessed," and the divine Logos stretches forth his hand to establish us upon the great waters.[7] This vision satisfies all that we might seek and desire, as "it exceeds the utmost imaginable degree of blessedness."[8] And what must be kept in mind is that "seeing" throughout Scripture carries the connotations of "possessing": "That you might behold the good things of Jerusalem" (Ps 128:5); "Let the impious person be taken away, that he may not behold the glory of the Lord" (Isa 26:10).[9] As Gregory concludes: "Will not he, then, who sees God possess, in this vision, every possible good thing: everlasting life, eternal imperishability,

4. Ibid., 30.
5. Ibid., 29.
6. Ibid..
7. Ibid., 30.
8. Ibid.
9. Ibid.

deathless blessedness, the true light, the sweet and spiritual voice, inaccessible glory, ceaseless exultation, and the ultimate good?"[10]

A Pure Heart?

Is it even possible to attain a "pure heart"? Who would step forward to admit such a thing? Gregory suggests that the saying is like the injunction that one must ascend to heaven, for it appears to be an unattainable and thus tragic demand: "Would the Lord really command us to do something that is beyond our nature and issue a commandment whose enormity oversteps our human capacity?"[11] And, if that true blessedness which is promised us in Christ is resultant from a vision of God, and that vision borne of a pure heart, one ought to understand purity as attainable.[12]

However, Gregory is insistent; the only true course of contemplation must be cognizant that God's nature "in and of itself, or essentially" is unapproachable.[13] When Paul incites the "unsearchable" and "inscrutable" ways of God (Rom 11:33), he recognizes the necessarily infinite distance between God and our conjectures or apprehensions of him.[14] For what mode of inquiry can render near that which is "beyond knowledge"?[15] God is "by nature, beyond all nature," he is invisible and uncircumscribed.[16] We, therefore, must look to other means if we are to apprehend him in any way at all.

Gregory employs the analogy of the artisan whose nature is perceptible through the thing made. And though his inscrutable essence remains opaque, we may know the wise nature of the one who so wisely made the "order of creation."[17] Moreover, the Christian witness of God's creative acts is telling of our nature as created

10. Ibid.
11. Ibid., 31.
12. Ibid., 32.
13. Ibid.
14. Ibid.
15. Ibid.
16. Ibid.
17. Ibid.

beings. For, we do not emanate by necessity from the divine perfection. Our being owes itself to the "free" and benevolent work of God, therefore we may comprehend his "goodness" if not his essence.[18]

Moreover, we may also apprehend the creator by tracing those high and lofty concepts toward their climactic and full glory. "Stamped on our souls" is the image of his attributes. And as we know the form or contour of "power," "purity," and "imperturbability" for instance, we may follow such things to their unhindered existence, their end and origin—the divine perfection.[19] It is in this way that Gregory sees it at once possible and impossible, necessary and unattainable, to "see" God; for we may not perceive his essence in itself, but we may know him who is invisible through his visible activities: he thus can be understood "analogically."[20]

A Type of "the Good"

However, this does not begin to explain why the "pure" are privileged in any sense over the natural observer of creations harmony. In order to understand this relationship Gregory turns to Jesus' words, "The kingdom of God is within you" (Luke 17:21). In attempting to contemplate the good things of God, the incarnate Logos instructs his followers to behold the divine nature in their own inner beauty: it is as though Jesus here says, "You human beings, who desire to contemplate what is truly good, do not despair of beholding the object of your desire just because you have heard that the divine majesty is exalted above the heavens, so that his glory is unsearchable, that his beauty is indescribable, and that his nature us incomprehensible. For that which is accessible, the measure of the contemplation of God, is within you."[21] Thus, Gregory says, we by nature share "essentially" in this good thing with the one who created us. We are called to cleanse ourselves from the

18. Ibid.
19. Ibid., 33.
20. Ibid.
21. Ibid., 34.

filth and obstruction that hinders the bright light of divine goodness. For in the cleansing of evil we apprehend our similarity to the "archetype" and thereby become "good": "For that which is similar to the good is assuredly good itself."[22]

And like seeing the sun by looking into a mirror, the blessed "beholds the archetype" by "beholding his own purity," for the one who "sees himself sees in himself that which he desires."[23] By freeing the image from corruption in our being we behold God in ourselves. However, searching for God in ourselves may ring out with curious and even nefarious tones—understanding this "seeing" as merely projecting; but Gregory makes such an argument not because of the independent and autonomous abilities of humanity, but because of a theological conviction borne of revelation that God alone is good. In perceiving goodness, even the minute instances, we are not to think that it stands on its own two feet as it were, nor are we to suppose that the goodness of creation is novel and self-sustaining. Rather, God alone is good ("You are my Lord; I have no good apart from you" [Ps 16:2]; cf. Luke 18:19); and by knowing goodness we begin to see God. And, "what is that blessed vision but purity, holiness, and simplicity, and all such luminous emanations of the divine nature through which God is known?"[24] God and the Good are properly simple, without division, gradation, or difference.

Gregory contrasts the good things of the soul with those "necessary" properties of passion in which we originate and "grow up."[25] Our natural constitution is one received—as like begets like—and we find ourselves ensnared by those passions which hinder the way of life. And yet this is not altogether surprising, Gregory finds in Jesus the expectation that the path toward the

22. Ibid.
23. Ibid.
24. Ibid., 35.
25. Ibid.

kingdom of God is "narrow and wearisome" while that path leading to "the performance of evil" runs "pleasantly and smoothly downhill."[26]

As Jesus makes explicit time and again, the old concern (primarily) with deeds is superseded by that which exists in the thoughts, the heart, the "inner" person. And what balances both the outward deeds and the inward feelings is the faculty of choice; it is in each instance a matter of choice whether that wicked thought is permitted to remain. In contrast to the law ("You have heard that is was said") Jesus commands that we put off the thought of anger: where we produce anger, he commands meekness. That anger taught by truth is subdued against our fellow and maintained toward sin and evil. With regard to the act of adultery, Jesus commands that we refuse to lust (Matt 5:28—even taking measures to accommodate our weakened flesh v. 29).[27] The old principle of an eye for an eye is muted by the command to submit to an evildoer (Matt 5:38–39), and he "cures our cowardice by commanding us to act disdainfully toward death" (cf. Matt 5:44).[28] By so attending to choice, Jesus unearths and squelches the seeds of wickedness within the heart. And as Gregory suggests, the tedious nature of good decisions is overshadowed only by the tedious and enslaving nature of poor decisions.

> Therefore, knowing by what means virtue and vice are formed, and since our free choice of the will enables us to choose either of these, let us flee from the image of the devil and put off that wicked mask. Instead, let us reassume the divine image, let us become pure in heart, that we may be blessed, the divine image being formed in us by pure conduct, in Christ Jesus our Lord, to whom be glory for ever and ever. Amen.[29]

---

26. Ibid.
27. Ibid., 37.
28. Ibid.
29. Ibid., 38.

Bibliography

Athanasius. *Selected Writings and Letters of Athanasius, Bishop of Alexandria*. Edited by Archibald Robertson. Nicene and Post-Nicene Father of the Christian Church, 2nd series, vol. 4. Edinburgh: T. & T. Clark, 1891.
Augustine. *Confessions: Books I–VIII*. Chicago: Great Books, 1955.
Balthasar, Hans Urs von. *Prayer*. San Francisco: Ignatius, 1986.
Barth, Karl. *Church Dogmatics: The Doctrine of the Word of God*. Edited by G.W. Bromiley and T. F. Torrance. Translated by G.W. Bromiley. Vol. 1/1. Peabody, MA: Hendrickson, 2010.
Bonhoeffer, Dietrich. *Christology*. New York: Harper & Row, 1966.
———. *Ethics*. New York: Macmillan, 1986.
———. *Life Together*. Translated by John W. Doberstein. New York: Harper & Row, 1954.
Brueggemann, Walter. *Awed to Heaven, Rooted in Earth: Prayers of Walter Brueggemann*. Philadelphia: Fortress, 2002.
Burns, J. Patout. *Theological Anthropology*. Philadelphia: Fortress, 1981.
Calvin, John. *Institutes of the Christian Religion*. Edited by Henry Beveridge. 2 vols. Grand Rapids: Eerdmans, 1989.
Gregory of Nyssa. *Select Writings and Letters of Gregory, Bishop of Nyssa*. Translated by William Moore and Henry Austin Wilson. Nicene and Post-Nicene Fathers of the Christian Church, 2nd series, vol. 5. Grand Rapids: Eerdmans, 1979.
Grimm, Harold J., ed. *Luther's Works: Career of the Reformer I*. Vol. 31. Philadelphia: Fortress, 1957.
Hart, David Bentley. *The Beauty of the Infinite: The Aesthetics of Christian Truth*. Grand Rapids: Eerdmans, 2003.
———. *The Experience of God: Being, Consciousness, Bliss*. New Haven: Yale University Press, 2013.
Heschel, Abraham Joshua. *God in Search of Man: A Philosophy of Judaism*. New York: Harper & Row, 1966.
———. *The Prophets*. New York: Harper & Row, 1969.
John of the Cross. *The Essential Writings: Selections from The Dark Night and Other Writings*. Edited by Emilie Griffin. Translated by Kieran Kavanaugh. San Francisco: HarperSanFrancisco, 2004.

Bibliography

Johnson, Keith L. *Karl Barth and the* Analogia Entis. London: T. & T. Clark, 2010.

Kempis, Thomas à. *The Imitation of Christ*. Translated by Aloysius Croft and Harold Bolton. Mineola, NY: Dover, 2003.

Lewis, C. S. *Mere Christianity*. In *The Complete C. S. Lewis Signature Classics*, 1–178. New York: HarperOne, 2007.

———. *The Screwtape Letters*. In *The Complete C. S. Lewis Signature Classics*, 179–296. New York: HarperOne, 2007.

McGinnis, Nicole M. *Draw Us after Thee: Daily Indulgenced Devotions for Catholics*. Bloomington, IN: iUniverse, 2012.

Moltmann, Jürgen. *The Crucified God: The Cross of Christ as the Foundation and Criticism of Christian Theology*. Minneapolis: Fortress, 1993.

———. *Theology of Hope: On the Ground and the Implications of a Christian Eschatology*. Minneapolis: Fortress, 1993.

www.ingramcontent.com/pod-product-compliance
Lightning Source LLC
Chambersburg PA
CBHW060409090426
42734CB00011B/2276